Simulated Stained Glass
for Amateurs

MAKING FRENGOSI WINDOWS FOR A WORSHIP CENTER

Simulated Stained Glass

for Amateurs

USING THE FRENGOSI METHOD

by

Ruth Case Almy

HARPER & BROTHERS · PUBLISHERS · NEW YORK

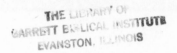

Contents

[v]

CONTENTS

*At the back of the book, following the Index, will be found
a working pattern sheet for two medallions.*

Plates*

* See Notes on Plates, p. 128, for the names of the artists and studios through whose courtesy these plates have been used.

Preface

THIS BOOK, AS THE TITLE IMPLIES, IS FOR AMATEURS. IT IS DIRECTED to amateur craftsmen who have longed to work with stained glass, but have found the processes involved too technical and the cost of the necessary tools prohibitive.

Other special groups will, it is hoped, find this book of use:

—Convalescent GIs and others interested in occupational therapy in hospitals and at home;

—Teachers of art in public and private schools who want a new and practical medium for illustrating the principles of design and color in relation to light;

—Teachers of religion who would acquaint children and young people with the art of praising God and telling of His wondrous works in terms of designed color-in-sunlight;

—Groups of young people who wish to use simulated stained glass as a background for a worship center, or to provide decoration in windows of a classroom or chapel;

—Architects, educators, and clergymen, who will find in it a simple, practical presentation of the subject of stained glass, about which there is a great lack of knowledge among most people of our day.

Frengosi (Trade Mark 440728 U.S. Patent Office) is the trade name of the method described here for simulating stained glass.

Frengosi glass as a term, is used to denote glass which has been treated by the Frengosi method.

(Bib. 1) in the text refers to the first book listed in the bibliography on page 121. Likewise, (Bib. 2) refers to the second book listed.

[ix]

Acknowledgments

THE AUTHOR WISHES TO THANK ALL THOSE STAINED GLASSMEN AND religious educators who have seen the educational possibilities in this venture and have been helpful in making this publication possible. We are especially indebted to Mr. Orin E. Skinner, Mr. Joseph G. Reynolds, Katharine Lamb, (Mrs. Trevor S. Tait), and Mr. Karl B. Lamb for reading the manuscript and making helpful suggestions; to Mr. I. Hurwitz for his personal help and counsel; to Betty G. James, public school art supervisor, Leonia, N. J.; and to those creative artists in stained glass who have graciously consented to the use of their designs for the illustrations in the text and for the supplementary pattern sheets (to be published separately and provided primarily for teachers of religion and young people who have little artistic ability or training).

It is hoped that amateurs who copy and adapt these stained glass designs, or create others in the same mode, will be stimulated to learn more about the mosaic, jewel-like masterpieces in Gothic cathedrals such as Chartres in France, and of the works of modern craftsmen who have successfully transplanted in America what has been called "the fresh loveliness of ancient windows."

Introduction

THERE HAVE BEEN MANY FEEBLE ATTEMPTS ON THE PART OF AMATEURS to simulate stained glass by means of oiled paper, painted muslin, or colored cellophane. The results are usually unsatisfactory because they are not based on the principles and techniques used in the stained glass craft. The author hopes that this process of simulating stained glass which she has chosen to call Frengosi (pronounced: *Fren-* as in French, *Go-* as in Gothic, *Si-* as in simulated) will be the means of introducing many to a firsthand knowledge of this unfamiliar field of art.

Most of us respond with sympathetic understanding when we view an artist's attempt to express himself on paper or canvas, because at some time in our lives we have made similar attempts. Pencils, crayons, water colors, and drawing paper are found on all toy counters, and are part of the play equipment of the average child. Anyone who has struggled at the piano with finger exercises, scales, fortes, and diminuendos, can better appreciate the skill and delicate interpretations of an accomplished pianist.

There is no such bond of common experience between us and the artist in stained glass. Our contact with glass is very limited, because it is usually associated with its breakage and the careful avoidance of the broken bits, lest we puncture a tire or sever a blood vessel. When a windowpane is broken we hire an expert to put in another, or if we replace it ourselves, we have the piece of glass cut to measure at the time of purchase. A glass cutter, sold in ten-cent stores, is an unfamiliar tool to most people.

We have all, no doubt, been thrilled at the sight of the dancing rainbow colors reflected from a glass prism in the sunlight. But it is safe to say that not one in a million has ever captured those colors in pieces of glass, cut them according to a designed pattern, and fastened them together with bands of lead, so that the rays of the sun can make them sing forth in a glorious harmony of light and color. Such are the daily privileges, pleasures, and problems of the worker with stained glass. Few amateur craftsmen and hobbyists have experimented in this field of art.

The Frengosi method of simulating stained glass eliminates cutting, firing, and leading together many pieces of colored glass. With black paper, a single sheet of a particular kind of glass, and selected paints, one is able to *approach* the same problems in design and color-in-light that were so successfully solved by the medieval craftsmen.

This simple, practical method of simulating stained glass can be a means of encouraging young and old to play creatively with color, in glass and light, just as they do with crayons, finger paints or modeling clay. Rays of light streaming through a medallion of his own making, as described in Chapter 4, will be a joy and delight to any amateur craftsman.

The Frengosi process of simulation has the encouragement of leading glassmen because they feel that here is a medium within the means and skill of amateurs, that will help to create public interest in their craft. It is hoped that Frengosi will be a practical link in the formation of a bond of common experience between amateurs and master craftsmen that will make for a better understanding and appreciation of this significant form of art.

Simulated stained glass can never take the place of *real* stained glass; but an attempt to master the techniques described here will enable one to develop a better understanding and appreciation of stained glass. Great windows in hundreds of our American churches can be studied and freely enjoyed by all. (See page 118 for a list of churches containing windows representative of the best in stained glass.) Churches in large cities and in many small towns contain just as much of interest to the informed observer as the museums, parks, and places of amusement. This publication will have served its purpose if it leads many to explore the "happy secrets of the gay and fascinating world of stained glass." "This region of glass-in-light is more like a fairy land than it is like a workaday world. The grandest windows are like articulate flowers, that speak as clearly as the flowers spoke to Alice in her looking glass world" (Bib. 3).

Part One

STAINED GLASS AND
THE FRENGOSI METHOD

Chapter 1

What Is Stained Glass?

ALL GLASS IS SAND, MELTED AND RUN TOGETHER. THE BEST GLASS IS made largely of silica, powdered quartz, or flint, which does not recrystallize while cooling, but forms a transparent substance that is plastic while hot. Pure sand can be melted only under great heat, 1000 to 1200 degrees Fahrenheit; but it can be made to melt at a lower temperature when a flux of potash or soda is added.

Glass is made into sheets by being blown into bubbles, just as a child blows soap or plastic bubbles. The blowing tube is dipped into the molten glass and a bubble is blown. The bubble is cut open at each end to form a tube. While still hot, this tube is cut down one side and spread out with tools upon a flat stone. The stone upon which the glass is flattened gives the surface of the glass.

The term "stained glass" technically applies to all glass that is colored in the pot while in a molten stage, by the addition of various metallic oxides. By common usage, stained glass is generally understood to signify windows. To most Americans the term means a design or picture made of pieces of colored glass held together with bands of lead and placed in a window opening.

Information on this subject in public libraries is classified under "Glass—staining and painting." Glass staining and glass painting are two different processes. It is customary to group them under one title because the two processes are used together in making stained glass windows. All stained glass windows are constructed of hundreds, sometimes thousands, of pieces of colored glass (called pot metal) fitted and bound together with grooved bands of lead, like a jigsaw puzzle, to conform to a plan. A small stained glass medallion or a large window, regardless of design or kind of glass used, is made by the same general method.

SIMULATED STAINED GLASS

FIRST STEP—THE COLORED SKETCH

The artist first obtains information as to the architectural style of the building, the exact dimensions of the window, and its particular position and function in the building. He then makes a small pen-and-ink

FIG. 1   Designing

sketch of a proposed window design, usually to the scale of one inch to one foot. Colors are indicated by water-color or tempera paint so as to convey an impression of the color and light of the finished window.

SECOND STEP—THE CARTOON

A full-sized charcoal drawing of the sketch, called the cartoon, is then made. This is drawn with great care and accuracy because it is

FIG. 2   Cartooning

the master pattern for the finished window. The positions of the iron crossbars and perpendicular supports (stanchions) so necessary to the

[4]

support of all leaded windows, are taken into account. The lead bands which hold each piece of glass in place are carefully outlined, and all lines that are to be painted on the glass to define features, drapery folds, shadings, and decorative patterns, are clearly indicated. If the window is very large the cartoon may be made in several sections.

Third Step—Working Drawing and Cutting Pattern

By means of carbon paper, two tracings of the leadlines of the cartoon are made on large sheets of plain paper. One is fastened on a table top and is called the working drawing. The other, of heavier paper, is cut up as a pattern for the individual pieces of glass. This cutting is done with double-bladed scissors which also cuts away a narrow strip of paper around each piece to allow for the lead band which will outline the pieces of glass and hold them together. Paper patterns thus cut are numbered and pinned in place on the working drawing.

Fig. 3   Patterning   Fig. 4   Cutting

Fourth Step—Selection and Cutting of Glass

The cutter, often a talented artist, selects with skill and care glass of various tones, textures, and shades, to match those indicated in the original colored sketch. He places the pattern on a piece of the desired color, and with a diamond or steel wheel cuts the glass to the shape of the pattern. Cutting of the glass requires technical skill; and, due to variations in the thickness, is not altogether simple even to one of experience. Raw edges are filed off for protection of the hands of workmen who handle the many pieces.

Fifth Step—Pieces Assembled Against the Light

When all pieces are cut, they are temporarily fastened with beeswax in their respective places on a plate glass easel, upon which has been painted in black the lead lines shown in the cartoon. This glass easel is then placed for further study in the same light, if possible, as will shine through the finished window when installed in its permanent position. Colors are changed and shifted until a satisfactory harmony and balance are achieved. The glass is then ready for painting.

Sixth Step—Painting

The work of the glass painter has much to do with the quality of the finished product. Unlike the painter in oils on canvas, who is only concerned with reflected light, he has to take into account the many changes in the play of light through each piece of glass. Light changes with every hour of the day and also with the seasons of the year. It comes and goes with every passing cloud, and varies with direct sunlight, clear or overcast skies, and reflected light from other objects. The painter on glass is faced with the ever-changing relationship between intensity of light and shade and depth of color.

Fig. 5   Painting

He uses a brown or black pigment made of metallic oxide and gum arabic, soluble in water, to define the forms and patterns indicated in the cartoon, and to bring out various tones and shades in the color. The paint is applied in bold brush strokes as he works on the glass easel against the light, or he lays each piece of glass over

[6]

the cartoon and traces the lines and patterns shown in the drawing. He also spreads a mat or halftone over some areas and allows it to dry. This mat is then stippled away or scratched off in lines and patterns to produce the desired effect.

Seventh Step—Firing and Annealing

When each piece of glass has been painted it is laid on a tray and placed in the kiln. Today firing is done with gas or electricity which makes for heat control never known in primitive kilns. The intense

Fig. 6   Firing

heat fuses the pigment properly and makes it a part of the glass. This process also requires technical skill and experience, for many different pieces of glass vary in quality and cannot all be treated alike. When firing is completed, the kiln is sealed and the glass is left to cool gradually. This is called "annealing."

Eighth Step—Repainting and Correction

After cooling, the glass is again put on the painter's easel for inspection. Individual parts may be too light or too dark or of an undesired shade, and new pieces must be cut, painted, and fired to replace them.

Ninth Step—Silver Staining

Silver stain is sometimes used to produce a clear, pure yellow color on glass, and usually requires a separate firing. Silver in powdered form is mixed with water or ammonia and generally painted on the back of the glass. It is fired at a lower temperature than that of the previous firing.

[7]

Tenth Step—Leading or Glazing

When painting and firing are completed, the glass pieces are ready for the glazier. He lays them on the working drawing and joins them with strips of flexible H-shaped lead bands called "cames" which look something like miniature girders. These lead strips, which are

Fig. 7   Glazing

placed around each piece of glass and frame each section of the window, are cut the desired length with a glazing knife and temporarily held in place with wire nails, inserted at intervals. They must conform to the pattern with great accuracy so that the completed window will fit the space for which it was designed.

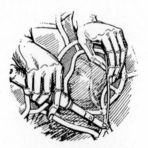

Fig. 8   Soldering

Eleventh Step—Soldering

All joints in the came are then soldered on both sides. Copper wires cut into short lengths are soldered to the lead wherever there will be an iron crossbar, so that when the window is installed these wires can be bound around the crossbars and twisted together to hold the window firmly in place.

TWELFTH STEP—CEMENTING

Cement is brushed into the spaces between the lead and glass, after which the edges of the leads are pressed down, the glass cleaned, and the window or section put aside until the cement is set. The cement

FIG. 9   Cementing

has properties which keep it from completely drying and flaking out. This adds to the resiliency that makes a good stained glass window stand against driving storms and varying temperature.

THIRTEENTH STEP—INSTALLATION

The final step in the process is fitting the window into place and fastening it to the supporting iron stanchions and crossbars that are set into the stone work. Often a window is put in place temporarily for the artist to see it in varying light conditions. At times changes and modifications in color must be made before satisfactory results are obtained.

All this is a long, slow process, and requires the artistic ability, technical knowledge, and experienced craftsmanship of many workmen. Risk of breaking involved in these many steps adds to the cost of production. A stained glass studio must be large and spacious, with suitable windows facing east, west, or south, so that artists may work with direct or indirect light. Therefore, overhead expense is an important factor in determining the cost of stained glass windows. Prices may range from a few hundreds to many thousands of dollars, de-

[9]

pending upon the quality and size of the various pieces of glass used, the type of design, skill of the artists, and reputation of the studio in which the work is done. The cost of a stained glass window should always be thought of in terms of permanence. A window made in a reputable studio will last as long as the building in which it is placed.

Chapter 2

Simulating Stained Glass by the Frengosi Method

WHEN ASKED WHAT IS MEANT BY THE PHRASE "TO SIMULATE" A young wit is said to have replied, "It is making something look like what it is when it ain't." Webster's definition of the verb simulate is, "To assume or have the mere appearance of, without the reality." Any method of simulating stained glass by using paper, cloth, or cellophane is usually unsatisfactory because these substitute materials cannot assume the "glassiness" of glass. The Frengosi method eliminates this handicap by the use of real glass.

The medieval glassman "was workman enough frankly to accept the limitations of his trade. He accommodated himself to the nature of his materials, never pretending to do what he could not, betraying neither the weakness of his materials nor his own" (Bib. 4). Makers of simulated stained glass must stay within the limitations of the craft and also abide by the further limitations of substitute materials and processes.

SIMULATION OF ANTIQUE COLORED GLASS.

A. Texture of Glass: Medieval glass was full of irregularities, striations, and bubbles. A modern inexpensive transparent glass that has some of the characteristics of antique glass is called *Velvex*. It is manufactured by the Blue Ridge Glass Co. and marketed by the Libby-Owens-Ford Co. It can be purchased from local glass dealers who carry their products. Velvex is a rolled glass, having the surface appearance of hammered brass or silver. The indentations are uneven and far enough apart to resemble somewhat the irregularities in old glass. It contains no bubbles or imperfections, but that is just one of the limitations which must be recognized and accepted. (See Plate

[11]

3a, following p. 30). If Velvex glass is not available, then English Double-Rolled glass can be used (see list of supplies, page 111).

B. Color in Glass: We do not mean to imitate any of the faults of stained glass in the sixteenth to nineteenth centuries described in Chapter 14, where we state: "No color applied to the surface of glass can have the limpid depth and luminosity of color suspended, as it were, within the glass itself." But with the Frengosi method it is necessary to paint the colors on the glass in order to avoid the very processes that are beyond the average skill of amateur craftsmen, namely, the cutting, firing, and leading together of many pieces of colored glass. The main problem therefore is to apply selected oil paints or Prang Dek-All colors to a single piece of clear textured glass so that each section, when colored, will *appear* to be a piece of stained glass or pot metal. The color is applied with a soft brush. The irregularities, streaks, and tone variations found in pot metal are simulated by brushwork or by patting and rubbing the color with a pad of cleansing tissue or air-foam rubber sponge. Directions for the application of the various colors are given in Chapter 5.

When using oil paints we are limited to those colors which are sunfast and transparent or semitransparent. Many pigments will give a lovely transparent color to glass but, due to their chemical content, will also fade when exposed for any length of time to the rays of the sun. The six oil colors listed on page 110 are the only ones known to be sunfast as well as transparent, and comprise a palette comparable to that used by the twelfth century glassmen.

Prang Dek-All is a newly developed color medium for the decoration of hard-surfaced objects, particularly glass. The colors are brilliant and very transparent when used with Dek-All Transparent Mix. This paint is thermo-setting and forms a permanent bond with the surface that is painted. The drying process can be speeded up and an extra degree of permanency produced by baking in a regular kitchen oven as specified in directions provided with Dek-All colors. Further information about this paint is given in chapter 5.

SIMULATION OF LEAD AND IRONWORK

The lead bands that surround each piece of glass are simulated with either a stencil cut out of black building paper or by painting

[12]

with black Dek-All paint. The black building or sheathing paper comes in rolls 36 inches wide at a reasonable price from any dealer in builders' supplies (see list of supplies on page 109). This paper is very easy to cut. Many amateurs, especially children, can cut a clean-edged line better than they paint one with a brush. The thickness, opacity, and surface texture of this paper make it desirable for simulating lead bands and iron crossbars. Outlines of the lead bands in a design are transferred from the cartoon to the black paper by means of white or yellow carbon paper. The spaces between the leads that represent glass are cut out with a pointed shears, razor blade cutter, or sharp knife. The resulting stencil of black paper is then glued to the rough surface of the Velvex glass.

Ironwork is simulated in the same way as lead. The paper bands may vary in width for thin or heavy bars, but will be wider than the bands representing lead.

Some may prefer to paint the lead lines on the glass with black Dek-All by fastening the cartoon firmly to the underside of the glass with Scotch Tape and painting the lines as they show through the glass.

Painting With Black on the Glass

In Frengosi, black paint on the colored glass is used in much the same manner as glassmen do to control the light and define the form. However, the black used is soluble in oil and therefore has certain limitations compared to the water-soluble pigment used in the stained glass craft. Painting with black in Frengosi is done only after the colored paint is thoroughly dry. For further explanation see Chapter 4.

Chapter 3

Suggestions for the Use of Frengosi Glass

A. Single Medallion as a Gift: The word medallion is here used for a unit of stained glass that may be round, square, rectangular, or diamond-shaped, varying in size from 6 to 25 inches. The design may be geometric or decorative, and include symbols or figures of religious or nonreligious significance (see Plate 1, following p. 30).

A colorful medallion of Frengosi glass makes an attractive gift. When hung in a window or suspended against the daylight it can be a source of constant pleasure as one watches its colors vary with the passing hours and changing seasons. Children as young as 9 or 10 years can do very acceptable work with a simple pattern such as found in the pattern sheet in the back of this book and the directions given in Chapter 4.

Florence, age ten, said, "My mother thinks my Frengosi medallion is the nicest gift I have ever made for her." And George's mother told how she had hung the medallion he made her for Christmas in every room in the house and then decided to leave it in the dining room where its varying moods could be enjoyed by every member of the family three times a day.

(Note: Other attractive gifts for children to make are the stained glass shade-pulls described on page 117, and the kaleidoscope on page 116.)

B. Individual Medallions for Instruction and Inspiration: The making of a Frengosi medallion is an excellent way to begin the study of stained glass and to stimulate interest in this unique form of art. In the church school, the designs may be an outgrowth of a study of the Bible, religious symbolism, worship, or missionary education. In the public school, the making of a medallion may be part of a course in color and design, or be correlated with studies in history, literature, the arts, or science.

In the church school, where the primary objective is to teach religion rather than drawing or design, it is advisable to furnish a pattern made by, or copied from one made by, an expert, so that the time, which is always at a premium, can be used to direct the children in producing that which will be a thing of beauty, a bit of "transfigured sunshine." Medallions or sections of favorite church windows can be reproduced and taken into the home or school to be enjoyed every day in the week.

Bob, who is ten, made a medallion at Christmas time showing the Christ Child wrapped in swaddling clothes, silhouetted against a blue background, and hung it in his bedroom window. One day he reported with a light of wonder in his eyes that he had watched the sunrise through his medallion and that some of the shades of blue had been turned to a beautiful deep purple. His parents said they overheard him explaining to his seven-year-old brother how the variations in the light out of doors made a difference in the colors of his medallion. It was this same boy who said, "I never paid much attention to the stained glass windows in our church until we began to do this."

C. Medallions as Window Decorations: Medallions may be placed in plain, paneled, or leaded windows, to provide interesting spots or bands of color. They may include figures and symbols that tell a story or convey a message to a certain age group or for a particular purpose or special occasion (see Plate 2, following p. 30).

There are some interesting medallions in the childrens' room of the Public Library in Englewood, N.J., where alternate rectangular sections of the windows are filled with stained glass designed by Margaret Redmond, of Boston, depicting well-known storybook characters. Sparkling, gay medallions designed by C. J. Connick, illustrating familiar characters in children's literature, cast their colored rays across the floor of the playroom of the Children's Hospital in Cincinnati, Ohio. Medallions and borders of Frengosi glass offer infinite possibilities for the addition of color and points of interest in windows of the school, church, hospital, public meeting

[15]

place, or home. Directions for adapting medallions to various types of windows are given on page 39.

D. *Medallions Set into Portable Panels:* Frengosi glass may be inserted in portable panels to be used as a background for a worship or interest center, as in the project developed in the Junior Department of the First Presbyterian Church of Englewood, N.J. (see Frontispiece or Plate 3b, following p. 30, and description of the project on page 112).

E. *Medallions Combined with a Decorative Background to Fill a Small Window:* Effective windows of Frengosi glass may be made by using medallions against a background of decorative grisaille or geometric diaper (see Plates 4 and 5, following p. 34). The making of such a window can be an interesting group project. The medallions can be made by those in the group who are most skilful with the brush, while every member of the group, even a child of eight years, can have a part in the painting of a simple background and border. For further details see Chapter 8.

F. *Windows in a Church, School, or Classroom:* Large windows filled with Frengosi glass of a simple grisaille pattern in suitable color can be used in a room to modify the light (see Plates 6 and 7, following p. 34). This is an inexpensive and practical way to provide temporary windows in a church in order to dispell surface light that may be destroying the effectiveness of a real stained glass window (see "Surface Light," p. 41). With proper care Frengosi glass can be preserved until permanent windows of stained glass are installed (see p. 41).

Amateurs are urged *not* to use Frengosi glass in large windows in a church, except in the grisaille pattern mentioned above. To make a design for a large window including full color and many figures requires the knowledge and skill of an expert. There are so many problems connected with the proper balancing of light, color, and form in a large window that amateurs with limited knowledge and skill are doomed to failure. The abominable windows of opalescent glass that desecrate many of our American churches are amateurish attempts to mimic the beautiful opalescent windows of John La Farge, who was a fine artist of the nineteenth century. It would be a worse desecration if churches were now decorated with crude imitation stained glass that is bound to disintegrate.

Amateurs will do well to confine their efforts to the making of Frengosi medallions and small windows in the home, church school or parish house, and leave large windows of the church to experts in stained glass. Most of us have some knowledge and skill in photography, and at times have taken pictures of our friends and loved ones. Occasionally we secure a likeness that merits an enlargement and perhaps a frame. But when we wish to have a really fine portrait we engage the services of a professional photographer or portrait painter. The making of Frengosi medallions or small windows for the church school can be the means of stimulating interest enough to make possible the raising of the necessary funds for securing the services of a professional craftsman to make real stained glass windows for the house of God.

G. *Dramatics:* If a stage setting calls for small stained glass windows (30 inches or less) they can be made of Frengosi glass and inserted in sections of the scenery. Large windows several feet high made of glass are not practical. The weight of the glass makes them difficult to handle and support in place. The lighting required to illuminate them properly poses a real problem for amateurs. In stage settings, the creation of an illusion is all that is really necessary. The *effect* of large stained glass windows can be obtained by using muslin or oiled paper, provided, of course, that the designs are based on the fundamental principles of good stained glass design. This is where most amateurs err. Their creations do not look like stained glass because their designs cannot be translated in terms of iron bars, lead, and glass.

When making stage windows, all of the suggestions and directions for making a simulated stained glass window with the Frengosi method can be followed, up to the point where the black stencil is glued on the glass. Instead, the stencil may be glued to muslin, heavy tracing paper, tracing cloth, or oiled paper stretched over a wooden frame. The parts of the muslin representing glass can be colored with watercolor paint. Oil paints can be used to color heavy tracing paper or tracing cloth, and enamel for oiled paper. The black lines and patterns, which are added on colored glass to define form and control light, can be painted on the muslin or paper with any opaque black that will adhere to the surface.

H. Experiment with New Forms: There is no reason for confining stained glass to religious subjects or to the Gothic form. However, the *character* of the Gothic is well worth keeping because of its respect for the limitations and inherent qualities of stained glass, its translucence and brilliance, and the laws of light and optics which no artist can ever change. Modern architectural forms and materials call for decorative glass to harmonize with their style. There are today several stained glassmen who have broken with the traditional forms and are applying modern design to the old medium or working with free patterns and abstract design in modern materials such as glass bricks and plate glass (see plate 8, following p. 30).

Chapter 4

Directions for Making a Frengosi Medallion and Reproducing Stained Glass Designs

PREPARATION

BEFORE AN AMATEUR CAN HOPE SUCCESSFULLY TO SIMULATE STAINED glass, he must be familiar with the nature of the materials and processes used by glassmen. Chapters 1, 2, and 7 to 15 will help one gain such information. However, it is impossible for anything written or pictured on paper to speak as eloquently as mosaic curtains of colored glass in sunlight.

Observe Colored Glass in Sunlight: Make it a point to see some excellent windows of Gothic stained glass (see list of representative windows mentioned on page 118). A trip of many miles if necessary will be well worth the effort involved. When a leader is taking a group to see some particular windows, it is wise for him to go to the place first to make arrangements for the visit of the group. He ought to know what stories the windows tell, the meaning of the symbols they contain, and ascertain the time of day they appear at their best. If possible, the group should see them at that hour. If such windows are nearby, several visits should be made to see them under conditions of varying light and weather. Where American art-glass or opalescent picture windows are found in the same place, their dull, static appearance may be contrasted with the lively brilliance of the jewel-like mosaic windows as they reflect patches of colored light on the floor or walls.

If it is possible to visit a stained glass studio, the same advance preparation should be made.

Some of the beauty of colored glass in sunlight may be observed

[19]

close at hand if scrap pieces of pot metal obtained from a stained glass studio are set up against a windowpane of clear glass. Avoid using opalescent or opaque glass. (See glass samples in the window above the boy shown in the frontispiece.)

The fascinating beauty and sparkle of varied patterns of colored glass can be observed through a kaleidoscope. Arrangements suitable for stained glass windows can be formed with a homemade kaleidoscope, or by replacing the tiny bits of colored glass usually found in a commercially manufactured one with larger pieces of pot metal (see directions on page 116). Designs observed in a kaleidoscope are of infinite variety, and no two are ever the same. With the slightest change in the position of one piece of glass within the toy, the complete pattern changes. Children can be trained to evaluate these designs if several kaleidoscopes are firmly supported so that each one can be observed by all, without moving the instrument. Combinations and balance of color can be varied by changing the size and color of the pieces in the kaleidoscope.

Make a Simple Beginning: It is better to begin by copying a simple medallion made by an expert than by attempting an original design for a whole window. The cartoons on the pattern sheet, in the back of this book have been provided with the understanding that they will be used in the same way that a boy making a model plane will use the diagram enclosed in the kit which he buys. The original design for a model plane is made by one skilled in the science of aeronautics. The proportions and construction are correct because they embody the laws and principles of aircraft engineering. These cartoons are the work of leading master craftsmen and embody the laws and principles of the stained glass craft. All problems in composition, design, and color have already been carefully worked out. When an amateur uses such a pattern for his first attempt he can direct all of his attention to the understanding and manipulation of his materials.

First Step—Cutting the Glass

Choose a simple cartoon such as those given on the pattern sheet and cut a piece of Velvex glass to the same size. It is advisable for

[20]

most amateurs to have glass cut to size at the time of purchase. Glass can be cut into circular shapes with the proper machine, and glass dealers who have such a device will give this service for a slight additional charge.

Glass is cut by running the steel wheel of a glass cutter over the glass with enough pressure to scratch the surface where the break is desired. If the wheel is dipped into kerosene before each cut is made, it works more easily. In order to cut a piece of glass accurately, lay the glass over a sheet of paper on which lines are drawn indicating the exact size the piece is to be. Then lay a straightedge, that is, a foot rule, T square, or anything that has a true edge, on the glass parallel with one of the lines on the paper. Run the glass cutter along the edge of it and over the glass. Start the glass cutter from the far edge of the glass and draw it towards you with a firm, even stroke. At the same time press down on it just enough to make it cut into or scratch the surface of the glass.

A glass cutter has several notches along its shank. Slip one of these notches over the edge of the glass after you have cut it; apply a little pressure, and the glass will break on the line you have cut. If it does not break easily, tap it gently with the handle of the cutter, on the underside of the glass along the scratch.

Second Step—Tracing the Pattern

If you choose to simulate the lead lines and crossbars with black paper, then lay the cartoon or pattern over a piece of black building paper of the same size as the cartoon (see list of materials, p. 109). Directions for simulating lead lines by painting them on the glass are given on page 13.

Fasten the black paper and the pattern to a drawing board or heavy cardboard with thumbtacks. Place the tacks along the top or one side, leaving the other sides free so that a sheet of white carbon paper can be slipped between them. If white carbon is not available, coat the back of the pattern with a light colored crayon or white chalk, brushing off all surplus chalk dust before tracing.

With a sharp pencil trace all the edges of the lead bands, indicated by the shaded portions in the cartoon. These lines will also form the outline of each section of glass. Check the tracing by lifting up one

[21]

side of the cartoon before removing the thumbtacks, to be sure that all lead lines or bands have been transferred.

Fig. 10   Tracing the Pattern

Third Step—Cutting the Black Paper

Remove the cartoon and the carbon and cut out of the black paper with a sharp knife or pointed scissors those portions of the design that represent glass. The remaining portions, representing lead bands and iron bars, will form a black stencil that is then ready to be glued to the glass. When copies of a cartoon can be mimeographed, each person

Fig. 11   Cutting the Black Stencil

can have two and the tracing process can be eliminated by cutting directly through the pattern and the black paper underneath. The second copy of the pattern is kept intact for use in tracing parts of the design to be painted in black, after the color is coated with varnish (steps 6 and 7). Directions for mimeographing patterns are given on page 32.

[22]

Fourth Step—Gluing the Stencil

Wash the glass thoroughly with warm water and soap to remove any oil or grease. Place the glass, *rough side up* on a sheet of newspaper. Place the black stencil, *topside down* on another sheet of newspaper. Apply the glue as evenly and quickly as possible. Carefully lift the stencil from the newspaper, turn it over, and lay it on the

Fig. 12   Gluing the Stencil to the Glass

rough surface of the glass. If the stencil is more than 15 inches square, it is wise to divide it into sections before applying the glue, by cutting through the center of a bar line. Press the stencil into place with the fingers and a damp cloth. When the black paper has everywhere adhered to the glass, remove any superfluous glue with a wet cloth. Turn the glass over and press out any air bubbles that can be seen from the underside.

If you prefer to paint the lead lines on the glass, fasten the cartoon firmly to the underside of the glass with Scotch Tape (be sure that the rougher surface of the Velvex glass is up). Paint in the lines as they appear through the glass. All lines painted should be perfectly opaque. Remove the cartoon and place the glass against the light. You may find that two coats of black may be necessary to achieve the proper degree of opacity. Dek-All black is recommended for this purpose because it is very opaque. When the black paint is dry, proceed to color the glass.

Fifth Step—Coloring the Glass

All directions in this chapter are general, and apply to the use of either oil paints or Prang Dek-All colors. In Chapter 5 detailed directions are given for the application of each color in both mediums.

The colored paint should be applied to the glass as it is held against the daylight. Racks for holding small panes of glass can be made out of wire coat hangers. Larger sheets of glass can be supported in a wooden framework (see wire holders and wooden horse shown in the frontispiece). An easel can also be made from a large picture frame. If several persons are working at the same time, and space at a window is not available to everyone, preliminary painting may be done over an electric light placed in a box or desk drawer. However,

FIG. 13   Painting the Glass

it is necessary to check all colors against the daylight and, if possible, light coming from the same direction as will shine through the medallion when it is finished and hung in place. Remember that the colors are transparent and will be influenced by reflected light from objects out of doors such as red walls, green grass, gray pavement, etc.

In addition to a rack or holder for supporting the glass against the daylight, each person should have a porcelain slab or saucer for a palette, and two small containers of turpentine. The turpentine in the first one is used only for moistening the brush and diluting the paint. It should be kept clean at all times. The second container is for turpentine which can be used over and over for cleaning the brushes. A glass jar used for baby food is good for this purpose. A small amount of clean turpentine can be kept in the lid and poured into the jar as it becomes dirty (see page 110 for other supplies needed).

The first step in applying color to the glass is to push or tuck the paint in well around the edges and into the corners of a section to be colored. In this way no tiny specks of clear light will be seen between the edge of the black paper and the colored areas. Do not worry about getting paint on the black stencil. Most colors will not show, except red, which can be painted over with black, or wiped off with a cotton applicator dipped in turpentine. After paint has been tucked in around the edges and into the corners, then paint the area just as you would a flat wall. Begin each stroke on the black paper and run it across the glass to the black paper on the opposite side. Use as few brush strokes as possible. Do not begin or end a brush stroke in the colored area as it will leave a brush mark and have a painted appearance rather than that of stained glass. Make all the brush strokes on

FIG. 14   Stippling the Color

one piece go in the same direction. Vary the direction of the strokes in the various pieces in order to simulate the irregularities and streaks found in pot metal, which are never alike or at the same angle in each piece. Scrap pieces of real stained glass should be kept before the individual or group for reference.

The light shades or tints of the various colors are easiest to apply. Dilute the paint with turpentine on the palette to the desired consistency and paint some of it around the edges of the portion to be colored. Then wash the paint on the rest of the area as you would a watercolor wash on paper.

Tints are also secured by painting the color on the glass, full strength, as it comes from the tube or jar and then rubbing it off with a pad of cotton or cleansing tissue held over the forefinger. Do not rub each piece in the same manner or direction. Always vary the manner of rubbing in order to simulate the variety in texture that

[25]

would be possible if each section were cut from a separate piece of colored glass.

Full deep tones are secured by applying the paint full strength and brushing it smooth with a wide brush, or stippling with a brush, rubber sponge, or soft tissue. The colors vary in texture and some techniques are more suited to one than to another (see Chapter 5).

Dek-All colors become set in a few hours and do not need a protective coat of varnish. When using them, omit the sixth step, "Varnishing" which only applies to oil paint, and proceed to the seventh step, "Painting with Black."

Oil paints on glass require several days to dry before the protective coat of varnish can be added. If time is limited, as in a conference lasting but a few days, a drying agent such as copra oil or Japan dryer can be mixed with the paint and turpentine.

SIXTH STEP—VARNISHING

When all colors on the glass are thoroughly dry, the whole thing, including the black paper, is given a coat of clear varnish. The varnish can be sprayed on with a fixative blower. If this is done,

FIG. 15   Varnishing

dilute the varnish with some turpentine in order to allow it to flow through the blower. Varnish can also be brushed on with a soft wide brush. Do not scrub with the brush or go over a place more than once, because the colors will begin to dissolve and lift off. Disregard any bubbles that may be formed as they will disappear in the drying or give a desirable texture to the glass if they remain.

It is possible to save some time by omitting the coat of varnish and painting the black lines and patterns directly over the color. This offers difficulties, however, as any corrections made on the black lines will loosen up the undercoat of color.

SEVENTH STEP—PAINTING WITH BLACK

Fasten the cartoon securely to the *underside* of the glass with Scotch Tape, and paint on the colored surface of the glass all the black lines and patterns indicated in the cartoon. Use firm, bold brush strokes. Most of these lines can be seen through the colored glass. They are seen more distinctly and are easier to trace if the glass is held against the daylight or over an electric light. The paper on which the cartoon is drawn can be made more translucent by rubbing it with oil.

FIG. 16   Painting with Black

When oil paints are used, the parts of the glass painted with ultramarine or Harrison red may be too opaque for the pattern to show through even with a strong light. If this is the case, place the cartoon *on top* of the glass and transfer those portions of the design that are indistinct to the varnished surface of the glass by means of black carbon paper. Press hard with the pencil when tracing these lines. If they cannot be seen clearly when transferred, dust them with a little white powder.

The black paint should be applied thin enough to flow evenly from the brush but thick enough to be a solid, opaque black. Much of the success in the use of black paint on glass depends on the kind of brush used. Red sable brushes are rather expensive but are more flexible than camel's hair or bristles and come to a better point than is ever obtainable with a cheap brush. It is advisable to invest in

[27]

several red sable brushes with good points and keep them just for painting with black.

When glassmen apply their black paint, which is soluble in water, they work from dark to light. If they want a light line or pattern to stand out against a background of black, they cover the entire area with black paint. When the pigment is dry they scratch or etch out lines with a sharp tool or the end of a brush handle. They secure a halftone by stippling the covered area with a stiff brush made for that purpose. Their black paint is easily wiped or brushed off before it is fired, to form the light portions of the design or pattern. Antique effects and interesting variations are often produced by flecking the stippled area with water. The pigment is then fused to the glass by firing.

The black oil paint or Dek-All color used in the Frengosi process cannot be manipulated in quite the same manner. In Frengosi it is easier to work from light to dark. All light portions of a design or pattern should be first outlined with black and then the background filled in around them. If the black is etched or scratched off when wet it is apt to smear; however, with a little patience and practice it can be done with the end of a brush handle or a toothpick. A tiny swab made of a bit of cotton on the end of a toothpick is a handy tool for lifting out light spots from a dark background or correcting and straightening black lines.

When all black lines and patterns in a design have been painted as accurately as possible, remove the cartoon and place the glass against the light. It will usually be necessary to touch up places that were missed, or where the black paint is thin and allows the light to shine through.

Eighth Step—Additional Painting to Modify the Color and Control the Light

Now, if possible, set your glass in the place for which it was designed, or where it can be viewed from the same distance and in the same light. You will probably find that due to halation or radiation of the various colors (see Chapter 7), many of the black lines are not bold enough. Some may even seem to disappear in the strong light. These will have to be strengthened and made heavier.

[28]

Some of the colors may be too thin or too brilliant in relation to others, and will tend to throw the design out of balance. These can be darkened with a thin application of additional color, or toned down by spattering them with black paint. Spattering is done by dipping an old tooth brush into thin black paint. Hold the bristle end of the brush close to the area to be spattered and with a toothpick or the stick end of a brush, scrape the bristles toward you and away from the glass. When the bristles snap back they will spatter tiny spots of black paint on the glass. By directing the spattering toward the edges and around the corners of a single colored section, the power or radiation of that color is reduced and the desired balance is secured.

FIG. 17   Additional Painting to Control the Light

"Patina" is the name given to the velvety coating or film found on very old stained glass windows, caused by the action of wind, rain, and the driving dust of the years. Bubbles near the surface of the glass become tiny pits whose shimmering walls have a great deal to do with the "mysterious quiet radiance of old windows" (Bib. 3). This desirable softening effect of patina and erosion is secured by modern glassmen by the use of acid and halftone mats flecked with water spots.

With the Frengosi process some semblance of patina and erosion can be secured by spattering black paint on the surface, as described above, or by painting a thin gray wash on the back of the glass. A gray wash should not be used to cover an entire section of glass, because it will destroy its brilliance. It is only used to shade a portion of the glass, to simulate the streaked appearance of pot metal, or to soften the edge of a black line where necessary.

[29]

Ninth Step—Finishing a Medallion

A medallion will look best if the edges are bound with real lead came (see supply list, p. 109). For a square or rectangular medallion cut the lead in lengths as long as each side of the glass, plus the width of the lead strip. Insert the glass in the groove along one side of the lead strip, leaving an equal portion of the lead extending beyond the glass at each end. Press the lead firmly to the glass and squeeze the ends of the lead strip until they are the same thickness as the glass.

Fig. 18   Soldering

Bind the opposite edge of the glass with another lead strip. In the same way bind the top and the bottom. Where the leads overlap at the corners, solder them firmly together on both sides. For a round medallion, cut the lead as long as the circumference, plus half the width of the lead for overlapping. Small screw eyes or wire loops can be soldered to the top or side leads for holding a wire or cord, by which the medallion is hung in the light. If the medallion is not too large and heavy, small holes can be pierced through the lead strip with a wire nail, and the cord or wire passed through them.

Strips of lead came are very soft and may become battered and bent. Before cutting into short lengths they should be straightened by stretching. Place one end of the strip in a vice. Grasp the other end firmly with a pair of pliers and pull.

Black passe partout or ordinary friction tape can be used instead of lead for binding the edges. If these are used, it will be necessary to construct a wire sling for holding the glass in the light. The wires of

Plate 1. SINGLE MEDALLIONS

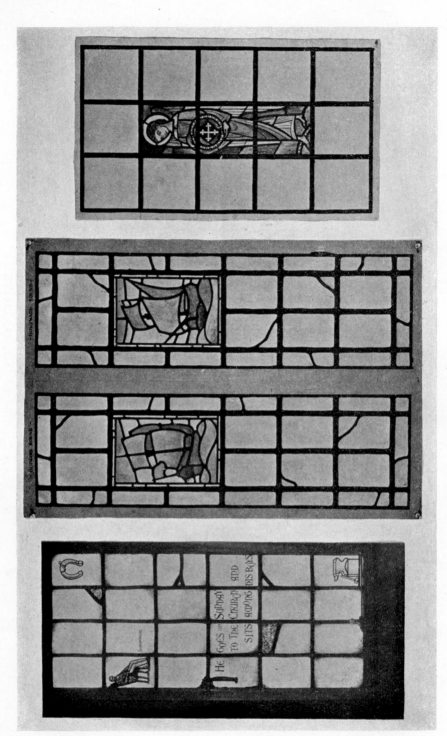

PLATE 2. MEDALLIONS IN A PLAIN LEADED WINDOW

A. VELVEX GLASS

B. FRENGOSI MEDALLIONS IN A PORTABLE
WORSHIP CENTER

PLATE 3

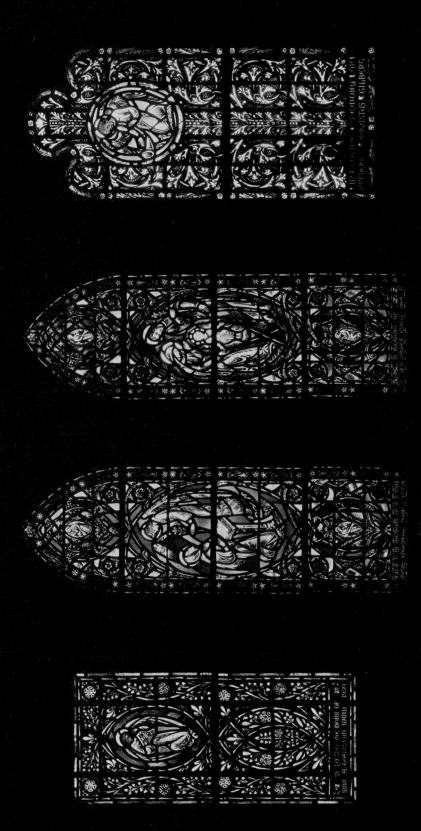

PLATE 4. SMALL WINDOWS WITH MEDALLIONS ON GRISAILLE BACKGROUND

PLATE 5.   SMALL WINDOWS WITH MEDALLIONS ON
BACKGROUND OF GEOMETRIC DESIGN

PLATE 6.   WINDOWS IN GRISAILLE WITH COLORED STRAPWORK

PLATE 7.   WINDOWS IN ORNAMENTAL GRISAILLE

PLATE 8. MODERN TRENDS IN STAINED GLASS

such a sling will not be noticeable if they are made to conform to the perpendicular lead lines or bars of the medallion.

If an amateur copies with care and accuracy a design made by a talented glassman, the finished medallion when hung in its place is never merely another piece of handwork. Even when made by the less skillful hands of a nine- or ten-year-old, it will possess a unique charm and beauty; beauty that is found only in active color-in-sunlight whose intensity and vibrance are effected by every passing hour and change of weather. It will sing out in joyous praise or glow in jewel-like splendor against the powerful rays of the sun because the design has been made for *light*, just as an arrangement of lines and notes by a musical composer is made for *sound*.

How to Make Patterns for Reproducing Stained Glass Designs

Many amateurs with little confidence in their own artistic ability may be content to confine themselves to the use of the patterns in the back of this book or those offered in the Frengosi pattern supplement to be published separately. Various color combinations can be used for the sake of variety. All of the patterns printed in the supplement may be copied for noncommercial use.

Religious educators, interested primarily in the teaching values of stained glass, may want to secure patterns for a particular medallion or portion of a favorite stained glass window. These can be made by tracing the design on heavy tracing paper held directly over the stained glass. If direct tracing is not possible, that portion of the window can be photographed and the picture enlarged to the required size. The camera should be placed high enough to avoid distortion of the design.

A design reproduced in an illustration can be photographed and enlarged to the desired size by the method mentioned above or by the use of a pantograph, or by the freehand method of blocking. A pantograph is an inexpensive gadget sold in stationery and artists' supply stores. With it a design may be traced any size, larger or smaller than the original. To enlarge or reduce a design by the freehand blocking method, simply draw lines on the design, dividing it into squares. Care should be taken to make all the squares perfect. Then lay out a similar shape in the desired size, and divide it into

[31]

an equal number of squares. Copy freehand the contents of each square.

Patterns or cartoons can be made on any firm, lightweight paper. White is preferable. After the design has been drawn in, paint all lead bands and iron bars with gray watercolor to differentiate them from the lines and patterns that are to be painted on the glass with black. These lines and patterns should be painted black on the cartoon with watercolor or India ink.

The mimeograph can be used to duplicate patterns. Trace the design on a mimeograph stencil. Outline with a fine stylus all the leads, bars, and portions to be painted in black. The leads and bars can be shaded gray by using a coarse shading screen. The painted portions can be made nearly black by using a very fine screen. See Chapter 8, p. 50, for further details about making the cartoons.

Chapter 5

How to Apply the Various Colors

THE FOLLOWING DIRECTIONS FOR OIL PAINT SHOULD BE SUPPLEMENTED by reference to page 35 for the use of Dek-All colors.

Red: Harrison red is permanent but only semitransparent, and is the most difficult of the colors to apply. The brush and turpentine must be kept perfectly clean or the color will be cloudy and dull. For this reason it is advisable to paint all red portions first. Apply the paint full strength. Push it into the corners and around the edges close to the black paper, and allow it to set for a few minutes. Then smooth it out with a flat brush, moistened in a little turpentine; or pat smooth with a finger covered with a piece of cleansing tissue. Irregularities and striations in red glass may be simulated by varying the brush strokes and manner of stippling. Feel free to experiment with different brushwork. Unsatisfactory results can always be removed with a soft cloth or piece of tissue. Care and patience are necessary to distribute the color evenly and avoid a "painted" appearance.

Due to its semitransparent nature, Harrison red should not be used for large areas such as backgrounds. This red will appear more brilliant when confined to small areas or heavily patterned with black paint. To have but one shade of red, and that not very transparent, is one of the limitations of Frengosi. But "reasonable limitations of any kind ought never to be considered as hindrances in any work of art. They are part of the problem" (Bib. 19).

Yellow Ocher: This color also has its limitations. It does not approach the clear brilliant yellow of silver stain, but is more like the yellow of pot metal. If applied too thick it will appear brown and opaque. It is more brilliant when surrounded by contrasting colors or confined to small areas and patterned with black. Apply it with a brush and stipple or pat smooth with your forefinger covered by a soft tissue.

Orange: Orange is made by mixing Harrison red and yellow ocher. It is a rather dull brownish-orange but is usable for small areas, particularly in borders, as a variation of red or yellow. Apply orange in the same way as red or yellow.

Green: Phthalocyanine or Monastral green, a new synthetic color, is a cool or bluish-green. It is transparent and can be painted on glass as easily as varnish. Apply it with a brush, using a broad flat stroke —daubing will destroy its brilliance. A warm yellow green can be obtained by mixing yellow ocher with Monastral green.

Blue: Ultramarine blue, like the Harrison red, is only semitransparent, but its powerful quality of radiation makes it suitable for larger areas in a design, such as backgrounds and borders. It may be applied just as it comes from the tube and patted smooth with a dauber. Care is needed to distribute the color evenly. If it is too thick it will stop the light and if too thin it will not be the deep rich tone of blue glass. A very light shade of ultramarine will give the glass a lavender cast which is usable as a tint or variation of white.
   Phthalocyanine or Monastral blue is a greenish-blue, transparent and brilliant. When applied with a wide flat brush it looks more like real stained glass than any of the other colors except the light tints. It may be used straight or mixed with ultramarine to give variation to a blue background or border. In the lighter shades it is beautiful for drapery.

Brown: Burnt umber is transparent and can be washed on with a brush. When mixed with yellow ocher to form a warm or yellowish-brown it must be patted smooth with a dauber. Burnt umber mixed with Harrison red will give a warm reddish-brown that must also be stippled or patted smooth.

Flesh: Flesh color is made by mixing burnt umber with a touch of yellow, red, or ultramarine blue, depending on the tone that is desired.

[34]

Yellow and red added to the brown will give it a warm cast, while ultramarine will give it a cold or purplish hue. Flesh that is surrounded with warm colors should be of a cool tone for contrast. Warm flesh tones are used in contrast to cold blues, greens, or whites. Avoid using a pinkish natural tint for flesh as it will appear weak and is too realistic for Gothic stained glass.

White: White glass is always a tint of some color. Glass left perfectly clear will appear gray and dull against the light, but will become brilliant with the addition of a touch of color. Warm whites are made with tints of red, yellow, yellow-green, yellowish-brown, and gray. Cool whites include tints of blue, blue-green, blueish-brown, and a lavender obtained by using a light tint of ultramarine.

It will be noted that no purple is listed, because no purple oil paint is transparent and at the same time permanent. The effect of purple may be obtained, as was so often done in the thirteenth century, by using red and blue in juxtaposition.

All colors may be darkened by allowing the first coat to dry and giving it a thin wash of the same or another color. Red may be darkened with a thin second application of red, but a coat of any other color will dull its brilliance. Ultramarine may also be darkened with a second coat of the same color or slightly varied with a wash of Monastral blue. Monastral blue may be given a greenish cast by the addition of a little Monastral green. Yellow may be varied by adding a wash of red, brown, or green.

DIRECTIONS FOR USING PRANG DEK-ALL COLORS

Prang Dek-All paints are a product of the American Crayon Co. They have just appeared on the market as this book goes to press and consequently the author has had only a short time to experiment with them with the Frengosi method. The following directions and comments are based on this limited experience and are subject to revision. The American Crayon Co. is planning to publish information pertaining to the use of this paint for simulating stained glass. Address inquiries to The American Crayon Co., Sandusky, Ohio.

The directions given in Chapter 4 for applying the colors to glass can be followed when using Dek-All paints, with the following exceptions:

1. Before any painting is done, the glass must be thoroughly cleansed of all oils or fingerprints by sponging it with a cleaning fluid such as Carbona or Energine.

2. A cotton pad or cleansing tissue cannot be used with Dek-All because it is more sticky than oil paint. All Dek-All colors are applied with a brush, and removed when necessary with a soft cloth dipped in turpentine. Any stippling that is needed to remove brush marks or to vary the texture of a section of glass can be done with a small piece of airfoam rubber sponge moistened in turpentine. A small piece of sponge is needed for each color.

3. Dek-All colors, with the exception of the blue, should not be applied on the glass just as they come from the jar. In order to simulate the various colors and shades typical of French Gothic stained glass, it is necessary to mix them in various combinations.

Dek-All Red: This red is quite transparent and therefore not subject to the limitations of Harrison red in oil paint. In order to obtain the various shades of ruby glass, Dek-All red must be mixed with either yellow or a little blue. If applied just as it comes from the jar it will give an undesirable cerise tone to the glass.

Dek-All Yellow: Mix a touch of red with this yellow in order to obtain the straw color of yellow pot metal. As it comes from the jar Dek-All yellow is more like the brassy yellow produced in stained glass by the use of silver stain. Yellow pot metal was always used sparingly in medieval windows, and silver stain was not known until the fifteenth century.

Dek-All Blue: There is only one shade of blue offered in Dek-All paint at present. The addition of a little green or red will vary the tone. Blue is the most difficult of the colors to apply. Deep rich tones are hard to obtain with the first application. However, they can be built up with one or more applications of a thin coat of color. Be sure the first coat is very dry before the second coat is added. Do not allow the blue to become so heavy that it is no longer transparent.

Beautiful shades of purple can be obtained by mixing Dek-All red and Dek-All blue. Shades of purple should be used sparingly, especially if combined with red, or the color effect will be hot and turgid.

Dek-All Green: This is a yellow green. It is necessary to add blue or a little brown to obtain a dark rich green.

Brown: As yet there is no ready-mixed brown in Dek-All colors but the manufacturer assures us that there will be one. The same directions given for the application of burnt umber in oil paints apply to Dek-All brown (see "Brown" and "Flesh," p. 34).

White: Various shades of white as described on page 35 are secured by mixing a touch of color with Dek-All Transparent Mix. *Do not* use the white Dek-All paint which is included in the sets of Dek-All colors when simulating stained glass.

Dek-All Black: This is used for painting all the black lines on the colored glass which define the form and control light. It can also be used to simulate the lead lines, in preference to the black paper stencil. Do not at any time add black to a color in order to darken it. All colors may be darkened by giving them an additional coat of the same or another color.

Dek-All paints are a product of modern scientific research. As in all new products, changes and improvements will be made from time to time in compliance with popular demand.

Adventuring in the Realm of Stained Glass
with the Frengosi Method

ANY AMATEUR WITH AN INQUIRING MIND AND A VENTURESOME SPIRIT
will find unlimited pleasure and satisfaction in exploring this fascinating realm of designed color-in-sunlight. In attempting to make an
original window design or adapt the works of others to a particular
place, several things are to be kept in mind.

First, "A stained glass window is an accessory to architecture"
(Bib. 19). It should appear as part of the flat wall surface and not
as a picture seen through an opening in the wall. With this in mind,
we must respect the work of the architect of a building by adapting
our design to the shape of the window as it now is. Most amateurs
think that a stained glass window is not churchlike unless it is arch-
shaped. They proceed to alter the top of a rectangular window with
an improvised arch, usually of the wrong curve and proportions.
They often add some sort of imitation tracery, the lines of which,
according to F. R. Webber, "Violate every principle of good proportion and design, and its detail is coarse and vulgar" (Bib. 48). This
is an affront to the architect, for parts of the window thus covered
may ruin the appearance of the building from the outside.

Second, the Frengosi method of simulating stained glass cannot be
successfully used on ordinary window glass. It must be used on
Velvex, or glass of a similar texture (see p. 11). Frengosi glass is
always used to cover or replace the plain window glass. Before a
design is made it should be determined just how the Frengosi glass
is to be used. It is wise to seek the technical advice of a local carpenter,
builder, architect, or capable handy man. Both the design and the
way in which the Frengosi glass will be used will depend largely on

[38]

the ability of the designer, the skill of those who execute the design on glass, and the amount of time and money at their disposal.

WAYS OF USING FRENGOSI GLASS IN VARIOUS TYPES OF WINDOWS

The easiest and most simple way to use Frengosi glass in an *Ordinary Window* is to hang in it a single medallion suspended by a wire or cord fastened to the window frame.

In a *Window of Plain Glass Divided into Several Sections* by strips of wood or metal, a Frengosi medallion can be used in one of the sections, and pieces of real stained glass of varying shapes can be fastened in some of the corners of the other sections to provide interesting spots of color. For a window with framework and divisions of wood, a medallion should be cut to fit snugly into the frame-work of a section. It can be held in place with glazier's points and putty, or by a narrow molding tacked to the wooden framework. Where frames and divisions are of metal, the medallions must first be framed in lead came and then soldered or wired to the metal framework. When this is done, the width of the lead came should be taken into account before the glass is cut.

Several medallions can be placed in a *Large Leaded Window*. If this is done, it is wise to take accurate measurements and make a paper pattern of each section to be covered, as they may appear to be the same but vary slightly in size. When planning for such a window, make a scaled drawing of the entire window, showing the divisions and proposed medallions in color. Medallions should be designed and placed so that the window as a whole will be pleasing in design and color arrangement. The monotony of lines and spaces in symmetrical sections can be overcome by the careful planning of the arrangement and proportions of the spots of color in relation to the clear areas which surround them. A medallion can be made larger than a single section of a window by extending the border over into the next section, or by adapting the design to include one or more of the crossbars. Variations in lines and spaces can be secured by introducing additional lead lines, real or simulated. Differently shaped pieces of colored glass bound on the edges with black tape or lead came, and placed here and there, help to overcome the sameness of uniform sections (see Plate 2, following p. 30).

Small Windows consisting of a single sheet of window glass can be covered with a sheet of Frengosi glass, cut to fit snugly inside the window frame and held in place with glazier's points, putty, or narrow molding. There is no limit to the form of such a window, as simulated crossbars and lead lines can be introduced anywhere the design seems to require them.

In *Large Windows* where it is necessary to fill the entire window in order to modify the light in a room, and it is not possible to cover all the sections with Frenosi glass because of expense or labor involved, medallions and perhaps a border of glass can be used in some of the sections and the rest of the window covered with simulated grisaille background made on heavy tracing paper or tracing cloth instead of glass. This grisaille background may be fastened to a wooden framework that fits over the entire window and provides openings through which the medallions can be seen. Small units of the border and background can be of pieces of scrap stained glass, inserted into the tracing paper or tracing cloth and taped in place to give the design sparkle and brilliance.

This treatment is being considered by one art teacher for the large windows in the school auditorium where the effect of stained glass is desired for festival occasions such as Christmas and Easter. The medallions and border are to be installed permanently and the rest of the window left clear, because the auditorium is used for a study hall every day. For special occasions when a more subdued light is desired, the background design, made on heavy tracing paper, and fastened to a wooden framework, will be set in place over each window.

Large windows used as a background for a worship or interest center may be covered with a panel of wallboard or plywood, and painted an appropriate color or covered with a suitable fabric, into which is inserted a large medallion of Frengosi glass. The Frengosi medallion can be held in place with a wooden molding. When a window is covered in this way for special occasions or used as a worship center only on Sunday, the background panel can be fastened to a framework of wood made so it can be set in place against the window and removed with a minimum of time and effort. The framework can be wired in place or fastened with small slide bolts (see frontispiece or Plate 3b, following p. 30, and project described on page 112).

It should be remembered that wooden framework should be put together with screws rather than nails, to minimize warping.

For some degree of permanence in windows, Frengosi glass may be sandwiched between the clear window glass and a covering of thin picture glass. This covering will protect the oil paint from being scratched off and the black paper from pulling away from the surface. The edges of the "sandwich" may be sealed with rubber cement or putty to prevent dust sifting between the layers. One hazard in covering a Frengosi window with picture glass is that it is apt to catch reflections that will ruin the stained glass effect.

Surface Light is the deadly enemy of stained glass, real or simulated. It is like the reflection on the surface of glass over a painting. Only as light streams *through* translucent windows are they expressive. Any opposing light or reflection which diminishes the flow of light through the glass, or stops it altogether, can turn the most glorious window into a thing which is dull and drab. If light strikes the inner surface of a stained glass window, it usually comes from glaring transparent windows near by or from those of colored glass that are too light for their place. When a window does not appear to be surrounded with a mass of deep gray or black, you may be sure that surface light is doing its deadly work. Curtains, shutters, or adequate temporary windows should be used to modify the offending light. When surface light is caused by artificial light a lighting engineer should be consulted about ways and means of its control.

After the mechanical problems of installing Frengosi glass have been worked out in detail, the next important consideration is *color*.

The choice of a general color scheme depends first of all on the amount of light desired in a room and the position of the window in relation to the sun. A north window in full rich color may make the room too dark, while too many lighter tints in an east or south window may be too bright. Colors should also be chosen to harmonize with the decorations in the room and to appear at their best at the time of day when seen by most people. Colors are affected by any reflected light or shadows cast by objects outside. Reflected light from a red brick wall will tend to change blue to purple, yellow to orange, and green to a brownish-gray. Reflected yellow light will dull the blues and warm the greens and reds.

These problems, and the many others that present themselves as one works with colored glass in sunlight, deserve most serious attention. A thorough understanding of how colors react to light and to each other requires knowledge and skill that comes only with diligent study and patient experimenting. Careful reading of Chapter 7 will give one an elementary knowledge of the basic laws of light and optics so successfully employed by medieval glassmen and used today by leading modern craftsmen. The "patient experimenting" need not frighten an amateur, because it can be a very pleasant adventure. The very fact that colors in a Frengosi window can easily be changed by removing the color with turpentine, ought to encourage anyone to launch out and follow the old adage, "If at first you don't succeed try, try again."

Colored Glass in Sunlight*

LIGHT PASSING THROUGH COLORED GLASS HAS THREE CHARACTERISTICS:
(1) it spreads or radiates; (2) it seems to eat up or devour black and
modifies contours; (3) it completely dies when opposed by a powerful
light shining upon the other side of the glass (see *Surface Light*,
p. 41).

Let us examine the first characteristic, that of radiation. The
radiation of light through different colors varies in activity and power.
A deep pure blue has more radiant power than any of the colors.
Red radiates less and yellow only a little if it tends toward a straw
color; not at all if it nears orange.

Radiation from blue glass, if uncontrolled, will fade and dull the
other colors. It is this luminous quality of blue, when properly con-
trolled, that gives a window light and life. A window in which there
is no blue will have a dull or harsh appearance. It may be said that the
success or failure of color harmony and balance in any window depends on the ability of the artist to control the blue.

The effect of the radiation of the blue upon adjacent colors is
illustrated in Figure 19, showing a section of a window composed
of undecorated or raw glass and leads.

The black lines represent lead. The squares are red and the circles,
blue. The bands which connect them are white. The blue in the
circles radiates over the other colors as far as the dotted lines as in *A*,
with the result that the corners of each red square become violet,
while only the center remains pure red. The ends of the white bands
appear blue and even the black leads in the area are tinged with
blue. When viewed from a distance the over-all color effect is purple.

---

* These observations and diagrams are based on the work of Viollet-le-Duc, as
translated by Holland (Bib. 16), and Smith (Bib. 17).

The radiation of the blue can be lessened by painting upon it a design in black as in *B*. This reduces radiation and there is less violet on the corners of the red squares. The radiation on the white bands can be further decreased by the use of pale green or a light yellow instead of the white. If these bands are also patterned with black lines or beading, the bands will stand out more distinctly against the background.

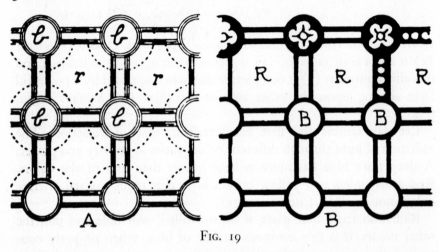

FIG. 19

Each color acquires its value only through the contrast with another color. For this reason no two pieces of colored glass of the same value are placed side by side. The many pieces that compose a large area of a single color should vary slightly in tone value and texture.

Colors not only influence each other, but each color is activated by light in its own way. This peculiar activity of light in the primary colors, red, yellow, and blue, is illustrated in Fig. 20.

Four square openings of equal size are made in a black background as *A*. In the first square is white glass, in the second is a deep pure blue, the third is a rich red approaching orange, and the fourth is a straw-colored yellow. It is presumed that the glass used is pot metal containing bubbles and striations. When these squares are viewed from a distance and in strong sunlight, the light shining through the white square tends to dart out at the corners, making the square seem larger than it is. Light shining through the blue square radiates or spreads

[44]

out in all directions, softens the edges of the square and gives the surrounding background a bluish cast. The red square will have a sharp
angular activity of light that breaks over the edges in a few places as

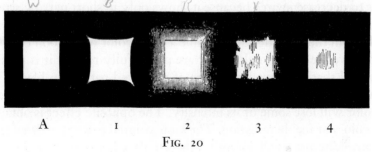

A   1   2   3   4

FIG. 20

indicated in the third square. The last square, which is yellow, holds
its edges firmly and retains its true size, but it seems to be of a deeper
tone at the center.

The secondary colors, which are green, purple, brown, and orange,
are a combination of two or more of the primary colors. They react in
light according to the characteristics of each component primary
color; a bluish-green, for instance, will have more radiation than a
yellowish-green.

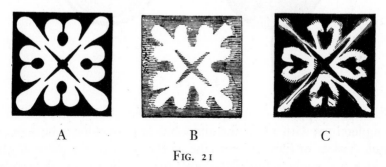

A   B   C

FIG. 21

These characteristics of light peculiar to certain colors are further
illustrated in Fig. 21, showing the action of light through a pattern of
black paint on red and blue glass.

If the pattern *A* is painted upon a piece of blue glass the power of
radiation is reduced, the edges of the pattern become blurred, and
the blue appears to be grayer, as in *B*.

[45]

If the same pattern *A* is painted on ruby glass containing streaks and irregularities, the pattern will tend to close in, or squeeze the color. When viewed from a distance the red becomes more intense and seems to decrease in area because it shows only in short narrow streaks or stabs of light as in *C*. If the red glass is of an even color and texture, it will from the same distance assume a wine color or maroon cast.

Thus we see that in colors that are powerfully radiant it is possible to control that radiance by the use of a painted pattern in black. The further off one goes the more indistinct the pattern will become and the color will lose some of its intensity. The opposite effect is obtained with colors of feeble radiation. The same painted pattern, viewed from the same distance, will intensify these colors because they are concentrated into the small areas that are left unpainted.

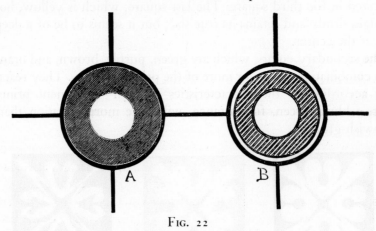

FIG. 22

Black paint applied to any piece of colored glass should not cover it completely as with a film, but allow bits of pure color to be seen. An opaque shadow or film will not take on the color of the piece of glass to which it is applied, but will absorb that of the surrounding colors in proportion to their power of radiation. This principle is illustrated in Fig. 22.

Here is a circle of red on a background of blue. If a gray shadow or film is painted over the entire area of red, it will not deepen the reddish tone of the glass, but will absorb the radiations from the surrounding background of blue. From a distance it will assume a dull

[46]

false tone which will be a mixture of brownish red and blue, that will deaden both colors, as in *A*.

If, as shown in *B*, the shadow is painted on by crosshatching instead of an even film, and at the same time the center and a narrow rim round the edge are left unpainted, then the pure red spaces between the hatchings and in the center will give the shadow a natural red tone, and the blue will maintain its own quality. An additional band of white, introduced between the red and the blue, will help them both to retain their true colors.

According to these principles, each piece of colored glass should be painted in conformity to its ability to radiate light and the influence of the colors that surround it. There is no set rule or formula for this. Every glassman develops his own style and technique in painting. After many years of experience with translucent glass in active light, he seems to know instinctively how to treat each piece. There are still many stained glass studios, however, where difficult problems of light and over-brilliant colors are solved by the generous use of a blanketing gray mat that stops the light. Their windows appear somber and dull in contrast to the sparkling jewel-like quality of windows made in studios where the above-mentioned principles are known and employed.

Amateur craftsmen can learn much by carefully observing at close range the various techniques and patterns used in painting fine stained glass. Opera glasses will help one to get a closer view when it is impossible to get very near to a window. (Much of the light radiations are lost or distorted when viewed through a lens.) Skill in the proper use of black paint on the various colors will come as a result of experience and experimentation. This is where the Frengosi method has a great advantage over the process used by stained glass artists. They can only alter the black painting on glass by adding more paint, which requires additional firing. If they find, after a piece has been fired, that too much black has been used, there is nothing to do but remove the piece, cut, paint, and refire another to take its place. With the Frengosi method, however, one needs merely to wipe off the paint with a little turpentine and repaint.

The second characteristic of light passing through glass is its ability to swallow up black. This is often seen in plain leaded windows where the leaded patterns look thin and in some cases seem to disappear. In simple leaded windows this difficulty is sometimes overcome by the use of rosettes or irregularities in the leads at points of intersection.

This power of sunlight to "eat up black" must be reckoned with in all designing for stained glass. It is particularly apparent in the hands and feet of a figure and in the features of a face. Fig 23 *A* is a hand as painted by a thirteenth-century craftsman. Had he drawn it on the glass true to nature, as in Fig. 23 *B*, from a distance it would appear as a confused flabby mass. By exaggerating the widths of the black between the fingers and accenting certain details, he preserved the silhouette and obtained the desired effect from a distance.

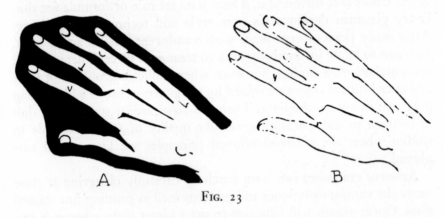

A   B

FIG. 23

Fig. 24 *A* is a thirteenth-century head, the original of which is about 18 inches high. It was designed for a large choir window of a great church and was therefore meant to be seen from a distance. The flesh is a light tint of warm purple, with greenish-white for the eyes. The hair is violet-purple and the crown yellow, with red and blue jewels. At a distance of 60 feet it takes on an entirely different character, as in Fig. 24 *B*. The lead joining the right eye to the nose disappears and many of the shadows are reduced to light halftones. The bold modeling of the right eye is greatly softened and the severe mouth and chin appear quite youthful. The careful and delicate modeling of the scratched-out highlights in the crown makes it a veritable jewel.

Light passing through glass not only makes black seem to disappear, but it also modifies the contour of a form. This is particularly noticeable in lettering on glass. Black lettering on a white background becomes confused and illegible at a short distance, while white letters on a black background can be read from a much greater distance. Because of the peculiar spreading characteristic of white (see Fig. 20, p. 45), the width of the letters should be very much less than one would presume necessary. This is why narrow bands and borders of white are heavily patterned or beaded so as to retain their firmness and form.

A   B

FIG. 24

These principles or laws governing the action of sunlight shining through stained glass will operate, though less effectively, with Frengosi glass if care has been taken to simulate striations and irregularities when the glass is colored. Actual models of Figures 19, 20, 21, and 22, made from stained glass scraps or Frengosi glass will be most helpful in demonstrating these facts. Such models made of stained glass need not be leaded together. The scraps of glass can be taped to the back of a black cardboard mask.

Chapter 8

Designing for Stained Glass

VERY OFTEN AN AMATEUR'S APPROACH TO STAINED GLASS DESIGN consists of selecting a simple picture, outlining its principal forms with heavy black lines, and breaking up the background area with a spider webbing of unrelated lines. This can be likened to an amateur musician who "composes" music by picking out a simple melody on the piano with one finger, while banging out a series of unrelated chords with the other hand.

To design for stained glass one needs a basic knowledge of the fundamental principles of good design. This book cannot include a treatise on design or the use of color; but several books on these subjects are listed in the bibliography. Amateurs will find "Design Approach to Crafts" particularly helpful. In it the author states "There can be no design except through expression in some kind of materials. There can be no craft worth doing without design." "True art expression in any medium depends upon the artist's command of design." (Bib. 52). Design is organization. It is the putting together of lines, shapes, forms, colors, and textures, in the finest possible way.

A stained glass window is designed color in sunlight. The primary function of a stained glass window is to admit and modify the light out of doors and at the same time exclude wind and weather. Designing for stained glass is the organization and putting together of shapes, forms, and colors by using iron work, leads, colored glass, and black paint. These should always be combined in accordance with the principles of good design as well as their functional purpose and inherent limitations. When designing for simulated stained glass there must be a further consideration of the possibilities and limitations of substitute materials. The ultimate test of a design made for stained glass, real or simulated, is whether or not it can be effectively translated in terms of

[50]

light shining through many pieces of colored glass held together by bands of lead and iron bars within a frame.

Iron Work

A leaded window is quite flexible, due to the softness of the lead. The pressure of wind and rain will cause it to bulge if it is not supported by strong crossbars provided at frequent intervals, usually about every nine to eighteen inches. In very wide windows vertical bars or stanchions are also needed. A medallion composed of many pieces of glass leaded together will sag with its own weight if it is not fastened to the iron work or firmly supported by wide leads. Study carefully the arrangement of iron work and medallions in Figure 31, p. 81).

Iron work should not interfere with the design, neither should it appear to be superimposed upon it. The iron work can give strength to the design by becoming an integral part of it. Stained glass men are usually free to arrange the cross bars to meet the needs of the design and the structural requirements of the window, but in adapting Frengosi glass to existing windows, the frame-work and other divisions are already in position. It is necessary, therefore, to make the design conform to these divisions. In Plate 3b, following p. 30, the designs for the medallions were adapted to fit the spaces formed by the horizontal and vertical bars of the large bay window left uncovered in the center of each panel. In Plate 7, following p. 30, we see how the iron work can be an integral part of the design.

The first step in making a small sketch for a single medallion, or a window, is to lay out accurately on paper the lines which represent the inner edge of the frame and the position of all existing divisions. In a small sketch these should be drawn to scale, using two inches to one foot. The next step is to create a design within the bounds of these limitations.

Leading

Lead cames are used to outline the form of the subject. The design is literally drawn with lines of lead, supplemented by black paint on the glass. These leads also determine the size, shape, and position of each mass of color, and are used to strengthen the structure of the

[51]

composition. In using lead cames to accomplish this, we must keep in mind the character and limitations of lead.

The strips of lead are made in various widths, from three sixteenths to one-half inch. The half inch width is usually used around the outer edge of a medallion, and to frame a window. In large windows, wide came is used to frame each section. The narrower widths are used within the design. Small pieces of glass are leaded with the narrow leads, and wider ones are used for the divisional lines. Leads are pliable, but it is not possible to bend them into sharp angles. Each lead is of uniform width, thus the edges are parallel throughout. This is to be remembered when simulating them with black paper.

"The leading of a window is the framework of its design, the skeleton to be filled out . . . and clothed in color; and if the anatomy is wrong, nothing will ever make the picture right" (Bib. 4). It is impossible, however, to think in terms of lead lines alone. One must also understand and constantly be aware of the function, purpose, and character of the other materials used. A musician composing a symphony knows the possibilities and limitations of the various instruments in the orchestra. He arranges a score for each one within the limits of staffs and bars which, when played in unison, will produce the harmony he has conceived. Just so, a designer for stained glass, while drawing with lead lines, is mindful of the possibilities and limitations of glass, color, and black paint, in relation to light and distance.

Because leads are used to outline the form of the subject, the choice of shapes and subject matter need careful consideration. The shape of a stained glass window is determined by the style of the architecture. Amateurs who use Frengosi glass in a window should work in harmony with the architect of a building, and not attempt, without his consent, to alter his work. The shape of a medallion will usually be determined by that of the space in which it is used. For practical reasons a single medallion of Frengosi glass will be square, diamond, or rectangular in shape. Round, oval, or star shaped designs can be used in these shapes if the corners are masked off with black or filled with appropriate ornament. The subject matter of a medallion or window can be religious, secular, or abstract, as shown in the illustrations in this book.

Regardless of the nature of the subject of a stained glass design, the principal objects portrayed should be reduced to their simplest form. Because of the action of light through transparent glass, contours are softened, details are lost, and colors seem to run together when viewed from a distance. The eye cannot distinguish the forms if they are confused or crowded together. Figures and symbols should be clearly silhouetted against a contrasting background. Avoid the crowding of figures. Make the background color appear frequently around them. The area of the background should be much less than that occupied by the figures. The movements and gestures of the figures should be strongly exaggerated or accented. It is best to show a figure in full front or side position. Foreshortened figures become headless, confused masses when viewed in light from a distance. All drawing should be sharp and vigorous. To avoid cramping or crowding, it may be necessary to allow a head, hand, foot, or piece of drapery to extend over into the border area. This is always done however in relation to the unity and balance of the design as a whole (see Plate 11, following p. 86).

The use of symbols is a great aid in simplifying a design. Rolling hills can be suggested by a curve at the horizon line. Trees and flowers by one or two examples in a conventionalized form, and water indicated by wavy lines of black paint on a field of blue (see Plate 11).

Lead lines should be sketched in at first with a medium soft pencil. Then place a piece of tracing paper over the drawing and trace the principal lines. Study them from the standpoint of proportion and design. See if any can be eliminated by shifting some of the forms and combining and simplifying others. Several tracings may be necessary before the resulting design is satisfactory. It must always be remembered that a lead line must completely surround each piece of glass and separate each color used, except in the case of abrasion in flash glass (see p. 93). Avoid lines which carry the eye off in the wrong direction. In a good design the lead lines are often unnoticed in the light, but a line in the wrong place is sure to attract attention.

When arranging lead lines in relation to pieces of glass, we must think in terms of the character and limitations of glass. Glass cannot be cut in sharp curves or angles without breaking. The crack usually

[53]

begins at the apex of the angle and runs to the nearest edge. This is avoided by introducing a lead line at this weakest point. The lead thus used adds strength to the structure and also makes it possible to vary the color by using two pieces of glass of a slightly different shade or texture. Notice in the clown medallion, (Plate 1, following p. 30) how lead lines have been used. The lines opposite the clown's ears strengthen the glass used for the background, and make it possible to introduce into the background a variety of shades and textures, instead of using a single color. In the Little Red Schoolhouse medallion on the same page, lead lines have been used across the deep curve in the path. If a sharp angle is needed in order to define a form, it can be painted in, as was done with the outer edge of the pathway leading to the Grecian temple in the Religious Liberty medallion, (Plate 1).

Long narrow strips of glass are to be avoided because they are structurally weak and the leads which surrounded them will be so close together that dust will collect between them and obstruct the flow of light. This problem is solved by making the strip of colored glass wider than it will appear in the design and then bringing it down to the proper width by the use of black paint. This is seen in the border around the clown's head, and in the Madonna and Child medallion, also in Plate 1. Narrow strips of color are sometimes obtained by means of black paint or abrasion. In the Battle of Lexington medallion, also on this page, the narrow line along the path or river separating the British from the Colonial soldiers is not leaded but painted on the same pieces of glass used for the grass. A strip such as this might be made white by etching it out of a piece of green flash glass. The same strip could be made yellow by applying silver stain to the white portion after it is etched.

Because leads are needed to separate each color used, sufficient space must be allowed in the design to accommodate them. This is another reason for keeping the design simple. Large areas in a design are broken up into pleasing spaces by the use of lead lines. The contrast caused by black lead lines and painted pattern in large patches of a single color, are needed to relieve the eye and add to the depth and brilliance of the color.

The space around a figure or form is usually divided by continuing the outline leads out to the border at the nearest point. There are exceptions however, when a line thus continued may weaken the structure or spoil the design. The lead line should never run directly into a corner. This would weaken the structure of the window.

Turn to the pattern sheet in the back of the book, and observe how the corners on pattern 1 are strengthened by the lead lines. The line which runs around the head of the giraffe on the right, and continues from his nose down past the leaves held in his mouth to the middle of his back, divides the blue sky at the point where it would be sure to break if made of a single piece of glass. It also carries the eye from the head of the giraffe down toward the children in the foreground. A similar line which meets the back of the giraffe on the left, is not a continuation of the head line, but of the left edge of the triangular piece on which the leaves are painted. It, too, strengthens the structure of the background and carries the eye in the general direction of the center of interest in the foreground. If the head line of this giraffe on the left had been continued the same as on the opposite side, the pieces of blue background on either side would be identical in form. The heart-shaped pattern thus formed by the leads in the center of the design would attract as much attention as the x-shaped pattern made by the yellow bodies of the giraffes. Variety in space and direction of line is also provided at the top of this medallion by the two leads that run from the necks of the giraffes to the upper border. The stone wall behind the central child is divided pleasantly into a variety of shapes which also make possible a variety in the brownish tones used for stones.

In the Nativity medallion (Pattern 2), the suggested form of a cross is preserved in the design by connecting the upper corners of the cross arm to the border at the nearest point. This tiny lead is completely lost in the light which radiates through the lighter colors of the glass forming the pattern of the cross. Notice also that the leads connecting the nimbus of Mary and the back of Joseph to the border, are not directly opposite each other. They vary somewhat and produce a variety of shapes in the background. The line which cuts across the triangle at the bottom of the medallion, does not run into the corner, but divides the area into two unequal parts at a pleasant angle and in keeping with other lines in the design.

[55]

Color

When we think of lead lines as determining the size, shape, and position of each block of color, we are faced with problems of the harmony and balance of transparent colors in relation to light as it shines through them. It is possible to experiment with various color arrangements by covering the sketch with a piece of tracing paper and blocking in the color with water color paint. These small traced sketches make it easier to judge the color scheme apart from the lead lines. In order to silhouette the figures or symbols against the background, masses of light colors should be used against a dark background, or dark colors against light backgrounds. Composite or secondary colors (green, brown, orange, and purple) are usually used against backgrounds of primary blue or red. Primary yellow is seldom used because of its great brilliance. Green is used occasionally for backgrounds and sections in a border. If primary colors are needed in the figures, they are used in smaller areas than those in the background, or isolated from the dominant primary color by a light tint or accent of white.

In Plate 3b, following p. 30, the figures in the four medallions are silhouetted against a background of ultramarine, and "Thalo" blues with the darker tones in the lower portions of the medallions where the design is most complicated. The robe of the Virgin in the first panel is also blue, but has a greenish cast, and is light enough to stand out from the blue of the background. The fur garment of the shepherd is brown, a secondary color, and is set off by the light tints of his scarf. The robe of the King is of primary red, but is separated from the blue background by the white bands of ermine trimming. The sections of border behind his shoulder are tints of white. The red of the robe worn by Jesus in the second and fourth medallions is set apart from the blue background by the light shades of his tunic. The primary blue and red used in the diamonds in the base of the first and fourth medallions are separated by bands of white and small squares of gold color. Before these sections of glass were patterned with black paint, the colors were thin and garish. After painting, the general color effect was that of rich purple relieved by sparkling accents of white and gold.

Amateurs will do well to study examples of fine stained glass

[56]

windows or colored reproductions such as those suggested in Bib. 1, 25, 26, and 27. Analyze various color combinations in relation to the basic principles given in chapter 7.

TEXTURE

Texture "is surface quality and is inherent in material. Different materials have differences in texture" (Bib. 52). The lead came, iron work, and glass are all hard materials and for the most part smooth. Surface texture of pot metal varies greatly in a single window; it may be mirror smooth, bumpy, pitted, streaked or wavy. When using the Frengosi method to simulate pot metal, we are limited to the texture of one piece of the Velvex glass and only such variations which can be simulated as colored paints are applied to it. Light of different intensities shining through these variations gives an added texture and quality to the glass that is only apparent to the eye. This texture is further enhanced by the application of black painted lines or patterns which in themselves control the action of light as it shines through the glass. The quality of a window is dependent upon the skill and interpretation of the artist craftsman.

Stained glass in sunlight, before it is painted, is called "raw glass." It can be compared to a musical composition when played according to the score but with no variations in the tempo or tone value. The addition of brush work, lines and patterns in black paint to the raw glass, is like the same musical score played by one who interprets it with all the skill and feeling of an artist. When planning a medallion or window, the designer is aware of the varied effects that can be secured in colored glass by the use of black paint. He cannot show many of these details in the small sketch. They will be partially worked out as the sketch is enlarged for the cartoon. Their final form is usually not determined until the actual painting is done on the glass against the light.

Before a sketch is enlarged for a full-sized cartoon, it should be criticized in relation to the principles of good design. Consider it first as simply a line drawing in black and white. Does it have rhythm, proportion, unity and balance? Are the forms defined as simply as possible in order to tell the story or convey the impression intended? View it from the standpoint of color alone, and see if there is proper dominance, balance, contrast, and harmony. Do the arrangement and proportion of the blocks or masses of color aid in telling the story?

THE CARTOON

The lines in a small sketch must all be doubled or enlarged in the cartoon to the actual width of the lead came to be used or simulated. There may be some question in the mind of the amateur as to just how this shall be done. Is the addition made on the inner or outer edge of the line, or is a little added on both sides? It may be done either way depending on the color, shape, and position in the design, of the piece of glass which it outlines. The actual size and form of an object is defined by the glass and not by the outline. In Pattern 1 on the pattern sheet in this book, the actual width of the arms and legs of the children is defined in the pieces of glass used for the flesh and the socks. The pieces of white glass used for socks are narrower than may seem necessary. This is because they are of white glass and the action of light through white glass will fill out the form (see Fig. 20, p. 45).

Stained glassmen do not make a distinction in their cartoons between the black which is lead and that which is painted on the glass. They know instinctively which is which. Amateurs are less confused if lead lines are painted dark gray to distinguish them from the painted lines in the pattern (see p. 32).

Detailed directions for adapting designs for particular types of windows can not be given here. The illustrations in this book have all been chosen with this practical application in mind. Study them carefully for suggestions.

SYMBOLS IN STAINED GLASS

A few words should be said here about the use of symbols, particularly Christian symbols, in designing for stained glass. "A symbol is an object or an action which represents an idea or a quality in something else. It should always be remembered that it is not a portrait." "The actual image is supposed to be like its subject, the symbol is not." "A symbol must be representative of something and not a representation" (Bib. 49).

Symbols should never be used simply because of their appropriate shape or attractive coloring. They are used only when they add to the meaning of a design or aid in telling a story. Those untrained in liturgical art must remember that "there is an ordered language of symbols just as there is an ordered language of words, and if we mix them we are quite likely to say what we do not mean." "To decorate a Unitarian church with triangles is like speaking Latin in Tokyo. If it is good to hear the Gospel read accurately in words, it is equally good to see the Gospel pictured accurately in symbols" (Bib. 49).

Several books on Christian symbolism are listed in the bibliography. When using symbols in stained glass design, it should be remembered that all pictorial presentations of symbols must be translated in terms of colored glass, lead, black paint and good design (see Fig. 40, at back of the book).

Part Two

HISTORY OF STAINED GLASS

Steps in the Development of Stained Glass

THERE ARE MANY LEGENDS CONCERNING THE ORIGIN OF GLASS. ONE says that the art of making glass was discovered by some Israelites who set fire to a forest. The heat became so great that it melted the sand and made it pour down the mountain (Bib. 38). Another, and perhaps the best known, tells of some shipwrecked Phoenician sailors who built a campfire on the fine white sands of an Assyrian beach. They used as a hearth some lumps of natron from the ship's cargo. Natron is a natural carbonate of soda, deposits of which were found in the Nile delta and used in ancient times for washing. These lumps of natron fluxed the hot sand to a molten mass, so that a pool of glass marked the campfire site the next morning (Bib. 34).

Glassmakers have an explanation of this story. They say that the campers probably burned the first thing they could find, which was a dried seaweed called kelp. The fire melted the fine white sand and as it mixed with the ashes it produced a thin film of glass. Old-school glassmakers insist that this could have happened if the fire had been hot enough, for kelp was used as a flux for centuries in making glass, as it contained sodium and potassium. Kelp also contained iodine, chlorine, and other elements that made trouble for the glassmaker, so that when chemists could furnish pure sodium and potassium, kelp was abandoned (Bib. 3).

Both of these tales have been discredited by those who say that no out-of-door fire could create the required amount of heat. But neither of these legends accounts for the earliest developments in glassmaking in various parts of the world. Glass objects recently found in the Euphrates region of Syria are said to date as far back as 2500 B.C., and small glass amulets found in Egypt date from 2000 B.C. (Bib. 34). The colors of the earliest Egyptian glass are soft and harmonious, often due to impurities such as lime, manganese, or traces of lead and zinc. Glass of extreme purity may have been known to the Chinese as long ago as 2300 B.C. for they were then using astronomical instruments, the lenses of which were presumably of glass (Bib. 4).

Beads of uncolored, transparent glass, resembling uncolored quartz, have been found in small quantities in Italian tombs of the eighth and ninth centuries B.C. These beads are of various sizes, generally as large as hazel-nuts, and are brilliantly transparent and without a trace of color (Bib. 34).

The first stained or colored transparent glass was made by the addition of various metallic oxides, such as copper, iron, and cobalt, to the glass when in a molten state. The art of imitating precious stones was known in ancient Egypt. Decorations and jewelry found in many tombs are a combination of real stones and glass imitations. It is said the Egyptians sent so many glass gems to India that they far outnumbered the real ones. The Indians sold them to other nations who came to buy the precious stones and knew no difference between the real and the false. It was glass, no doubt, that deceived many ancient travelers who told of jeweled thrones and great palaces set with gems.

The early glassmaker had little interest in window glass, probably because in his mild climate there was no need for protection from the weather. Window openings were often filled with stone lattice for protection against thieves, or with ornamental wood or plaster-work for decoration.

The first glass windows were made by setting bits of glass or small shells into these stone or plaster openings. The next step may have been the substitution of strips of lead, copper, or bronze for the heavy plaster. For centuries windows were made of small pieces of glass held together in some such fashion, for glass in large sheets was not made until the sixteenth century. As civilization spread northward into colder countries, glass windows played an important part in the economic, social, and religious life of the people, especially in regions where winters were long and the weather stormy.

When the persecution of Christians ceased in Rome in 313 A.D. and it was no longer necessary for them to gather secretly for worship in the Catacombs, many church buildings were erected, often directly over the old secret entrance to an underground chapel. These first churches were patterned after the Roman basilicas of that day. Early records state that the arched window openings were sometimes filled with slabs of marble which were pierced, and glass, not necessarily colored, put into the openings (Bib. 4).

Windows at Saint Sophia, at Constantinople (627 A.D.), were said to have been filled with colored glass set in alabaster, and were described by one as "exceeding in splendor anything that had been before seen." Another wrote, "It appears that day took its birth under the roof of the temple" (Bib. 3).

Windows of colored glass were mentioned in the fifth century by Jerome, and in the sixth century by Gregory of Tours. The Anglo-Saxon Chronicle tells of Bede introducing glass to England in the seventh century. These early windows were no doubt simple mosaics of colored glass held together with bands of lead, copper, or bronze. Men who fashioned windows out of small pieces of glass and bands of lead were called glaziers. They were often clever craftsmen and masters of good proportion and design.

There developed at Constantinople and Limoges, prior to the tenth century, a form of enameling called "cloisonné." Narrow strips of metal were soldered edgeways to a groundwork, and spaces between them filled with colored enamel made of glass ground to a fine powder. This enamel was fused to the groundwork at a low temperature in a furnace. Thus each color was separated by a thin metal strip which made the style of the design developed for cloisonné suitable also for glass. Venetian enamelers came to France in the tenth century and about that time the art of the glazier was united with that of the enameler and became the art of "stained and painted glass."

With the use of black or dark brown enamel it was possible to paint human forms on glass, and by decorative brushwork to control the light and enrich the color effects. This accounts for the rather sudden appearance of figures in windows. They were first mentioned by the Bishop of Rheims, who rebuilt his cathedral in 969 to 988 A.D. and decorated it with legendary windows.

A monastic chronicler in 1052 tells of a window, illustrating the martyrdom of a certain saint, that was placed in his chapel, having been transferred from an older church built in 820, shortly after the death of Charlemagne (Bib. 18). Another record tells of the furnishing of the first Benedictine monastery at Monte Cassino with a whole series of legendary windows in 1066 (Bib. 4).

By 1134 there seems to have been an overproduction of windows of colored glass, because the Cistercian Interdict restricted that particu-

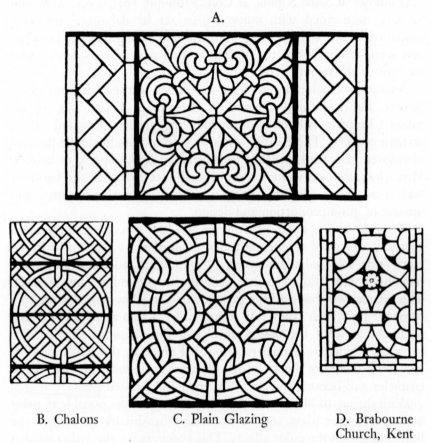

A.

B. Chalons   C. Plain Glazing   D. Brabourne
Church, Kent

Fig. 25

lar religious order to the use of white glass only. This led to the production of a type of design still known as "Cistercian," which consists of interesting patterns in lead and glass of varying texture and pale tints. Glass of this period was never pure white. These early craftsmen could not produce clear white glass as we know it today,

[66]

due to the impurities in the sand which they did not know how to eliminate.

Windows at the Abbey Church of Saint Denis that escaped destruction during the French Revolution may be considered among the most ancient now in existence. Here, in 1140 under the inspiration of Abbé Suger, the Gothic arch was born (Bib. 28). Until then most large buildings were of the Romanesque style and windows were limited in size by the width of the half-round arch. The Romans needed every foot of their heavy walls to hold up the roof. With the strong ribs of the Gothic arch and the comparatively light pillars and buttresses that would carry safely great roof weight, it was possible to have larger wall openings and to set them at a greater height.

Abbé Suger was a prominent religious leader of his day and a capable statesman. He was also a great builder and patron of the arts. While constructing the Abbey, he gathered about him large numbers of workers, artists, and craftsmen of every sort, including skillful makers of stained glass windows. It is said he originated many of the symbols used in the windows and supervised much of the work himself. His accounts give a detailed record of windows he had constructed, as he said, "To direct thought by material means toward that which is immaterial." The congregation was so interested in this work that the collection box placed in the church for the support of the artists was always full (Bib. 1).

After building the church at Saint Denis, these trained workers, many of whom had previous experience under the Cluniac monks, moved to Noyon, Sens, and on to Paris, where the Cathedral of Notre Dame was under construction. From there they went to Chartres where it might be said that Gothic architecture burst into full bloom, and stained glass such as in the "Tree of Jesse" window has been unrivaled to this day.

During the latter part of the twelfth and the beginning of the thirteenth centuries, ten great cathedrals were built in that part of France which has been spoken of as, "The lovely garden of the Gothic, where all Europe came to borrow seeds and slips" (Bib. 28). These noble structures are some of the finest artistic achievements the world has ever seen. Their works of art were not so much "art for art's sake," but rather for the propagation of the Christian faith. As the church carried on its missionary work in these centuries it could not depend upon the printed page which did not then exist; nor upon the spoken word, because no one knew how to procure satisfactory acoustics in large buildings. Therefore the church resorted to the use of symbols in wood, stone, painting, and stained glass. Every church was like a great picture book, expressing Christian history and current religious beliefs in a way that all might see and easily understand.

Their religion was a passion with them, so much so that kings and princes laid aside their royal finery, and peasants left their plows in the fields. All worked side by side from dawn until dark, dragging great stones to the hilltop where a mighty cathedral was being erected. Artisans would work for months strapped to scaffolding, carving delicate symbols, perhaps to be seen only by the organ tuner as he climbed the runway sixty feet above the choir steps (Bib. 47). Every gift or act of service was a symbol of religious fervor and devotion.

Archbishop Hugo of Rouen tells how the faithful citizens of Chartres and his own diocese "formed associations for the construction of their church by transporting the materials. They admitted no one into their company unless he had been to confession, had renounced enmities and revenges, and had reconciled himself with his enemies. They elected a chief, under whose direction they conducted their wagons in silence and humility" (Bib. 29).

At the request of the Bishop, King Philippe Auguste set aside a season for contributions and mass work on the Cathedral of Notre Dame in Paris. The people came from the countryside to join those in the city, and everyone, rich or poor, brought what he could. Wagons donated by farmers and the Guild of the Paris Waggoners were loaded with stone, iron, timber, and lime, or with supplies of meat, grain, and wine for the workers. Often it took as many as nine yoke of oxen to draw a single cart heavily laden with building stone. Other carts were drawn by knights and nobles who harnessed themselves to them. Often the rich and expensively dressed were yoked with the very poor and ragged. Even the children, laughing with the joy of it, brought their tiny carts filled with pebbles, in imitation of the building stones in the huge lumbering wagons.

[68]

The king and his queen rode to the square to greet the people as they gathered in as impressive and practical a pageant as the world has ever seen. Prayers of consecration and dedication were offered and, amid the waving banners and flickering torches, the sound of trumpets and mighty hymns went rolling up the hills (Bib. 28).

Stained glass windows and other works of art born out of such missionary zeal were made primarily for the glory of God and not for money or fame. The artist seldom signed his work nor was mention made of the donor.

This wonderful period continued for about two hundred years. It saw most of the great European cathedrals built; and produced such outstanding characters as St. Bernard, St. Francis, St. Dominic, and St. Louis. Then a reaction set in and there was a marked change in mental attitudes. Never again do we find a whole people, from princes to ploughmen, neglecting their own affairs and working side by side to build and decorate a glorious house of God (Bib. 13).

Churchmen living in the beauty and luxury of these great buildings grew comfortable and indifferent, and in some cases even selfish and corrupt. Laymen became either uninformed or uninterested in religion and often critical of it. The religious zeal which inspired the building and decorating of beautiful places for worship was not followed up by an effective program of religious education. Subsequent generations which grew up did not know or understand the original meaning of these symbols and works of art. Misinformation and abuses increased until the leaders of the Protestant Reformation declared all such things idolatrous and demanded their removal and destruction.

The stained glass windows which escaped the destructive hands of the reformers are today considered among the most priceless works of art ever created by the hands of men.

▰▰▰ Chapter 10 ▰▰▰

Stained Glass in the Twelfth Century

MASTER CRAFTSMEN IN GLASS SPEAK OF THE TWELFTH AND EARLY thirteenth century as "the golden days of the craft." J. G. Reynolds, writing for the *American Architectural Review*, says, "It was an age in which individual masterpieces were produced; marvelous in design, glorious in color, with a charm that even today holds us spell-bound" (Bib. 21).

FIG. 26   A Twelfth Century Worker

We moderns with a flare for psychology view one of these masterpieces and begin to ask questions about the man who was its creator. What did he look like? What was his philosophy of life? What was the secret of his power? A glassman of that period has been described as "an artist, a poet, and a gentleman; the only worker with his hands who at times was permitted to marry a royal lady. . . . Like all real poets, they knew the heart of their medium . . . and used it for praise and prayer, not just as a means of making money. When poets, worshipers and good workmen unite to exalt the spirit, through the use of material, miracles can happen" (Bib. 3). And they did.

Every craftsman was a master of his primitive tools and skilled in each step of the process, from making the colored glass to fitting the finished window within the stone wall. Windows for the most part were made on the building site. Workmen rented lodgings or pitched tents in the vicinity and set up their crucibles and whitened boards in the very shadow of the cathedral.

Colored glass, or pot metal, was made in fireproof clay pots by the addition of metallic oxides to the molten mass while in process of fusion. Chromium was used to make green or yellow, manganese for violet, and copper or gold for red. Red obtained from copper filings thrown into the mixture, together with flaked iron, was so rich and intense in color that light could not penetrate the entire thickness of the glass, and so the color was used as a thin red film plated on a clear glass. This was called "flashed" glass. The glass blower dipped his rod into molten white glass, and then into ruby, so that the knob of white glass was coated with ruby. When this was blown out it became a piece of thick white glass covered with a thin layer of ruby which was often very unequal in thickness and streaked in character. Flashed glass of other colors was not used until the fifteenth century.

White glass was never pure white, but varied from cool greens and blues to pale yellows, reds, and tans. Many of these tints were probably accidental. Then, as now, the making of colored glass was greatly dependent on the element of chance. In spite of special formulas, the same oxide often produced different colors with different glass mixtures. The degree and amount of heat applied to the mixture was also a determining factor in making various colors.

Theophilus, an early glassmaker, wrote, "If you notice a pot of melted glass turning yellow, let it boil for three hours and you will have a clear yellow. If you wish, let boil for six hours and you will have a red yellow. If you notice however, that the pot is turning reddish so that it resembles flesh, take from it, and use it for flesh color. Boil the rest for two hours and you will have a bright purple, and another three hours, and a real red" (Bib. 14).

Abbé Suger, another early authority, tells of the crushing and melting of many sapphires to make blue glass. Modern glassmakers believe he referred to nuggets of blue Venetian glass that added quality to the color in the melting pot, or to cobalt in a very pure form which is still used in making blue glass. Rubies and emeralds have in the same way been associated with other colors in glass. The names Ruby, Sapphire, and Emerald are used today as trade names for glass in sheets.

Early pot metal was of two kinds; muff or sheet glass, and crown glass. Sheet glass was made by gathering some molten glass onto the end of the blowing tube and shaping the mass on a marble slab. The workman blew until he formed a cylinder, then cut it off at both ends and opened it along its axis with a piece of hot iron. It was then reheated and spread out flat with the help of tongs.

Crown glass was made by blowing the glass into a flattened sphere, and fastening an iron rod called the punty onto the side opposite the blowing tube. The tube was then broken off and the opening thus obtained was widened by turning the glass rapidly in front of the furnace. Centrifugal force slowly opened up the spheroid which became a plate about eighteen inches in diameter, thicker at the center than at the side. This difference in thickness, causing a greater or lesser intensity of color, was very ably used by the glassmen to obtain color gradations and to relieve the monotony of the backgrounds (Bib. 1). Glass made in this way was full of air bubbles, flaws, bumps, and irregularities which broke up the sun's rays and made the glass sparkle.

The uniquely charming quality of antique glass is in this sparkle or active translucence. Tiny transparent spots serve to keep areas of color alive in light. Lewis Day says, "Try to describe the effect of an early mosaic window and you are compelled to liken it to jewelry. Jeweled is the only term which expresses it" (Bib. 4).

Original designs for these ancient windows were probably made on parchment and colored in a manner similar to illuminated manuscripts. The drawing would be considered crude by our standards. However, it was not an affected crudity, but rather an expression of the way they felt about things. Paper in large sheets was not known, so the full-sized cartoons were made on a flat wooden board or table covered with chalk. This also served for the cutting and glazing bench (see Fig. 26, p. 70). No mention is made in early writings on stained glass of the use of a glass easel, but it is difficult to imagine how the smallest

FIG. 27   Crucifixion Window, Poitiers

window could have been developed without one. Although pieces of white glass were small and irregular in shape, tinted with various shades of green, blue, and yellow, and full of bubbles and striations, they might have made a sort of easel by leading together the largest and whitest of these pieces. One writer speaks of glass temporarily

[73]

arranged in chassis or sash frames against the light, but he does not say how they were made or how the glass was held within them (Bib. 15). It is possible that the artists knew colored glass and its action in light so well that they felt no need of an easel.

These ancient craftsmen must have had an understanding of the activity of light that we now call scientific—a body of knowledge learned by the trial and error method over a long period of time. Mr. J. G. Reynolds calls attention to one master colorist in the great Crucifixion window in Poitiers (see Fig. 27, p. 73). "The hair of the crucified Christ is blue. But being placed as it is on a white and gold halo and surrounded with a large quantity of intense blue, the color of the hair is not noticed. It is safe to say that if it were any other color it would be noticed and would look wrong. On the other hand, the hair of the Ascending Christ is a rich brownish-purple. But the nimbus in this case is blue with a white cross. Instead of realism, the medieval glass worker sought decorative effect, choosing splendor of color rather than stolid facts of tint or hue" (Bib. 21).

When we consider the intricate patterns of those early windows, especially in the borders, we marvel at the skill with which the glass was cut or rather divided. Diamond glass cutters were not known until the seventeenth century. Theophilus, writing in the twelfth century, says in his directions to glass cutters: "Heat in the fire the dividing iron which should be thin throughout, but thicker at the end. When it glows in the thick part apply it to the glass which you wish to divide, and presently a small fissure will appear. If the glass be hard, wet it with saliva with your finger, in the place where you place the iron. As soon as it is cracked, draw the iron along where you wish to divide the glass and the crack will follow the iron" (Bib. 14).

The early glassmen laid each piece of glass to be cut over the drawing on the whitened board and followed the lines with the red hot iron. Later, patterns were cut from parchment, wooden board, or thin sheets of metal. The same cartoon or set of patterns was often used for several figures, as in the choir windows at Chartres. The colors are so varied that only the most careful observer is conscious of the resemblance in design.

According to Theophilus, the twelfth-century glass painter made his own brushes from the hair of the tail of the martin, badger, squirrel, or cat, or from the mane of an ass. These were crude at best. For fine lines he often used the feather of a wood cock. His pigment was similar to that used today. The direct bold nature of the brushwork of that

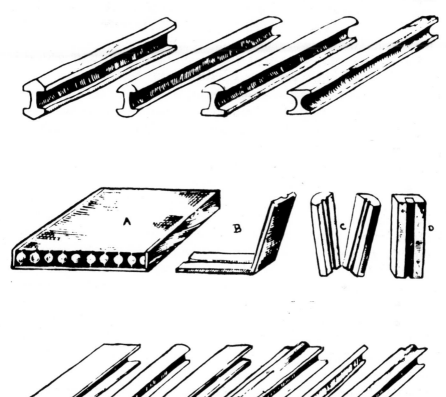

FIG. 28

(Top) Ancient lead cames. (Middle) Probable variations of ancient molds. A. Mold made by laying a number of round twigs side by side in a box and pouring the lead around them. B. A hinged iron mold. C. A wooden mold. D. A frame holding a bar of square-shaped lead to be grooved with a plane. (Bottom) Modern cames

period leads us to believe that not many details were drawn on the whitened board, but that the artist worked out his effects on the glass and created as he proceeded.

Early kilns were very primitive. They were made of arch-shaped iron rods covered with clay. Through holes near the base, other rods were placed crossways to support an iron plate above the fire, upon which the glass was laid. The glass was "burnt" over a beach fire. When it was thought to be hot enough, the fire was removed and the kiln left to cool. The exact degree of heat could not be measured and the results were always doubtful. When the glass was cool, or annealed, the paint was tested. If it could be scratched off with the fingernail it was fired again.

Lead cames for the glazier were made of pure tin and a sixth part lead. Round twigs were laid side by side within a wooden box to form a mold, and the melted lead was poured around them. Some lead was molded into square-shaped bars and grooved with a plane. Fitting these crude cames to pieces of glass, which were rough and irregular and varied in thickness, required great patience and skill.

Theophilus' instructions on window making ended with the soldering of the leads on both sides. He says nothing about cementing, nor of the ironwork to which the window sections were fastened. These directions were written long before the days of movable type and printing. All copies were laboriously made by hand. It is possible that some parts were left out by a copyist who may have thought them unnecessary, especially if the craft were popular.

The twelfth-century glassmen not only mastered their tools and materials, but they knew the principles of design and how to balance active color in light. It is this unique balance of color that makes twelfth-century windows so effective in all variations of light. Mr. Connick beautifully describes the central choir windows at Chartres as "pealing forth warm waves of color that recall vast passages for the bass viols, brasses, and woodwinds, in a gorgeous symphony. They have areas where the blues and reds mingle in red-violets, but such raucous influences are delayed, sometimes stopped, by passages of lively whites. . . . Those cooling whites not only keep that group of windows from turning shrill and ugly, they bring forth the warm melting beauty of the whole composition as a silver brook blesses the hot glow of an autumn field in sunlight. Those windows always look as though the sun was shining through them. On the grayest rainy days they hold the sunlight of radiant yesterdays" (Bib. 3).

Chartres is the only European cathedral which is lighted by prac-

A. The "Beautiful Window,"
Chartres

B. The Tree of Jesse Window,
Chartres

Fig. 29

tically all of its original windows. Their colors have been deepened and enriched with age. It has been said that to open the portals of this great church is like opening the very gates of Heaven, and to be there at the twilight hour when the reds and yellows in the windows disappear and all that remains is that mysterious veil of blue, is a spiritual experience (Bib. 22). The most popular windows in Chartres are the "Notre Dame de la Belle Verrière"* in the south ambulatory, often referred to as "The Beautiful Window" (see Fig. 29A), and the "Tree of Jesse" window in the western wall, which is considered by many to be *The* window of all time (see Fig. 29B, p. 77).

* A beautiful reproduction in color of a portion of this window is available for 25¢ (see Bib. 24).

Chapter 11

Stained Glass in the Thirteenth Century

FRENCH GOTHIC GLASS, ACCORDING TO WINSTON'S CLASSIFICATIONS, may be divided into three groups: Early Gothic, Middle Gothic, and Late Gothic (Bib. 20). He includes in the Early Gothic period the twelfth and thirteenth centuries. Some authorities speak of the twelfth century and those preceding it as the Byzantine or Romanesque period, and classify only the thirteenth century as Early Gothic. These divisions are all more or less arbitrary because one style merges into another and characteristics of one period overlap those of another.

Artists in the thirteenth century continued for the most part to make windows in the traditional forms of the twelfth century. However, they cared less for pure design and were more interested in telling stories in glass. Windows of this first period were of four kinds:

1. PATTERN WINDOWS

These were of purely decorative design, often in comparatively colorless glass such as the "Cistercian" (see Fig. 25, p. 66) and "grisaille," (pronounced griss-eye, see Fig. 33, p. 84). The designs for these early windows can be read by the lead lines alone. Little or no paint was used. They were Byzantine in character and resembled other designs of the time still preserved in marble mosaic, inlay, or appliqué embroidery.

2. FIGURE WINDOWS

Large single figures, or one above the other, were rich in color against a background of contrasting color. Saints and other personages were shown standing or sitting under some sort of architectural canopy. These canopies occurred throughout the three Gothic periods and into the Renaissance period which followed. At first they were small in comparison to the rest of the design. No attempt was made to show perspective. The saints faced front with their feet resting on little mounds of green which represent the earth, or on a straight label bearing their name.* Names or legends were sometimes scratched in bold Lombardi (white letters on black) on bands held in the hands or incorporated in the background. These figures are all rather stiff and very much alike. The clinging folds of drapery through which the limbs are plainly seen is Byzantine in style. In some of the figures white

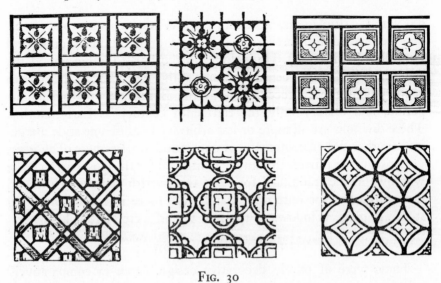

FIG. 30

glass is introduced for the eyes, which glare at one out of dark brownish-pink faces. A reddish-brown flesh color is characteristic of this period as it was the only flesh color they knew how to make.

3. MEDALLION WINDOWS

At first, the space in a window between the borders was divided into rectangular sections by means of crossbars and stanchions. Each of these square or oblong spaces was treated as a picture panel, framed by lines of white and color. Later, pictures in medallion form were arranged against a background of scrollwork, foliage, ornament, or geometric design (see Plate 9, following p. 86 and Figures 30, 31).

* Colored reproductions of such figures in early windows are available for 25¢ (see Bib. 27).

Backgrounds of geometric diaper utilized the many precious bits of glass that accumulated. In many of these windows the strong iron bars supporting the glass were bent by the blacksmith to follow the outlines of the medallions (see Fig. 31, and Plate 10, following p. 86). Figures in the medallions were few and far apart, silhouetted against a

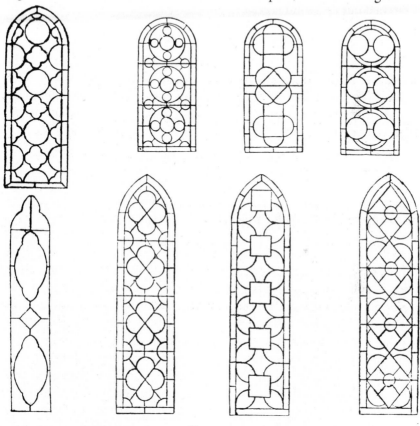

FIG. 31

plain background of blue or red, with borders of beaded white or solid color. Occasionally a halo, head, hand, foot, or piece of drapery extended into the border. Landscape was symbolized by a conventional tree, buildings were represented by an arch or two, and towns or cities by a section of battlemented wall (see Plate 11).

Black or brown paint was used to bring out details such as features of the face, fingers of a hand, folds of drapery, or decorative forms

[81]

such as leaves, flowers, and buds. Lines and crosshatchings were used to modify the color and regulate the amount of light shining through. A thin smear of paint was used to soften the solid lines and provide a tint which prevented the spreading of light. Paint was never used as color except in the case of hair, when curls and other details were scratched out of a solid layer of pigment with the stick end of a brush.

4. ROSE OR WHEEL WINDOWS

These are a variation of the medallion window and occur mainly in France. In the cathedrals of Chartres and Bourges they are a series of radiating medallion lights. The smaller rose windows often contain a circular medallion in the center and the cusps or foils around it are filled with richly colored ornament (see Plate 12, following p. 86).

5. TREE OF JESSE WINDOWS

The subject of these windows is always the genealogy of our Lord beginning with Jesse, the father of King David. The tree and figures are portrayed in symbolic and decorative form (see Fig. 29B, p. 77).

BORDERS

Borders were important features in early windows. At first they were very broad, one-fourth the width or one-half the area of the window. They consisted of geometric figures or foliated ornament and sometimes included small figure medallions. In figure and canopy windows the borders were narrower and more simple, often being just broad bands of color broken by rosettes of other colors. In rose windows the borders are not so important and are usually confined to the outer rims of a window section. Toward the end of the thirteenth century borders became narrower and interlacing stems and palmettes replaced the earlier forms of budding leaves and berries (see Fig. 32, p. 83).

Drawing in the thirteenth century was vigorous and more lifelike than that of the previous century. Richer and more varied colors were developed and there was a growing fondness for red. It is said that the glassmen became so absorbed in their great color symphonies that at times they forgot not only earlier traditions of light, but the actual light of day itself (Bib. 3).

[82]

Fig. 32   Typical Thirteenth Century Borders

FIG. 33   Grisaille Windows

GRISAILLE

Windows of grisaille, meaning gray, developed in the latter part of the thirteenth century, and probably came with an attempt to get more light into the dark, gloomy interiors. They were made of so-called "white" glass which was of varying tints, with cool greens predominating. The design was a trellis pattern made by the overlapping or interlacing of bands or strapwork in glass. A design of foliated scrolls was traced in bold brush strokes upon the areas between the bands, and the background was crosshatched with fine or coarse lines according to the distance from which the window was to be observed. In this way the pattern was made to stand out clearly against a background which had the appearance of a grayish tint. But the tiny transparent spaces between the cross hatchings gave it great brilliance, and the whole effect is that of a silvery luster.

In some of the earliest known grisaille windows (in Saint Denis near Paris, at Saint-Rémy Reims, and Salisbury), colors are introduced into the strapwork. Interlacing bands of color are paralleled by bands of white. These bands are not glazed separately, but are defined on the same pieces of glass that contain the crosshatched design (see Fig. 33, p. 84. The most famous grisaille windows are in the north transept of York Minster in England. These windows form a huge five-paneled screen of silvery glass, and are known as the "Five Sisters." They have been described "as beautiful as a spider's web, beaded with dew drops, glistening in the sun on a frosty winter's morning" (Bib. 5). Toward the end of the thirteenth century grisaille was used as a background for large figures in brilliant color. This became a very popular form in the fourteenth century.

The palette of the early glassmen was limited, but there was a great variety in shades due to the uncertain and accidental features in making glass. These shades ranged from near white to deep rich tones. Red usually had a ruby quality but, when streaked with white, ran close to orange. Mulberry, or maroon-brown, ranged from a light brown or tan to a brownish-red-violet. This color combined well with brilliant reds and blues, and added great charm to many early windows. Yellows were strong and deep, not brassy, but running often to orange. Yellow made by silver stain was pure, clear, and lemon in color.

Greens were pure as emerald, deep and velvety as moss, or of a somber olive tint (Bib. 4).

Whole chapters could be written about the blues of the middle ages. They ranged from turquoise, aquamarine, sapphire, cobalt, and ultramarine to soft gray blues. Pliny called the limpid true blue "the most beautiful color in the world." It is surely the most distinctive color of old windows, particularly of the thirteenth century.

The characteristics of the Early Gothic period could be summarized as follows (Bib. 13):

1. Its rich color (barbaric richness)
2. Its mosaic character
3. The importance of the iron-work and its influence on the design
4. The method of painting vigorous lines in black or brown enamel, and white letters scratched out of black*

* The order of these characteristics, as set forth by Saint and Arnold in *Stained Glass of the Middle Ages in England and France*, has been rearranged here to correspond to the order in which they are taken up in this book.

PLATE 9.   MEDALLION WINDOWS WITH BACKGROUND
OF SCROLLWORK AND GEOMETRIC DESIGN

PLATE 10.   MEDALLION WINDOWS WITH BENT ARMATURES

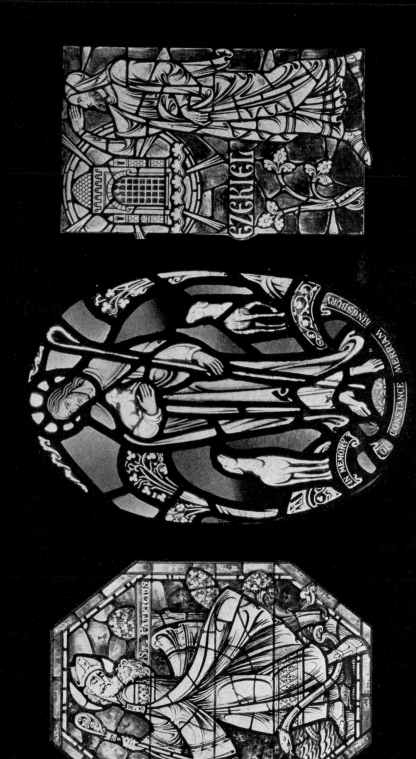

PLATE 11. SELECTED MEDALLIONS

PLATE 12.　ROSE WINDOW AND WHEEL WINDOW

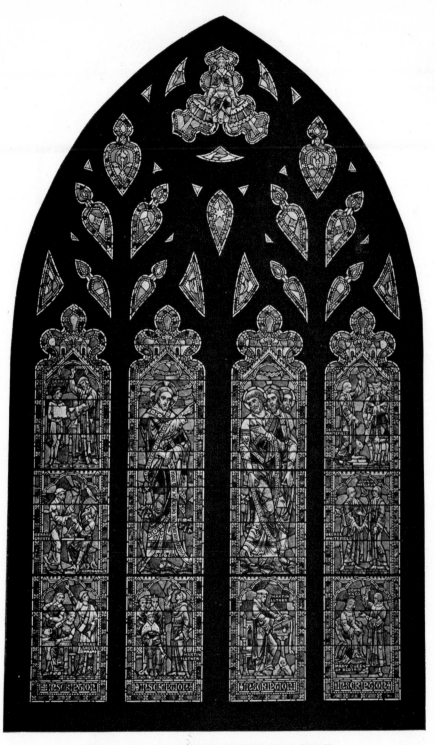

PLATE 13.   LANCETS WITH TRACERY

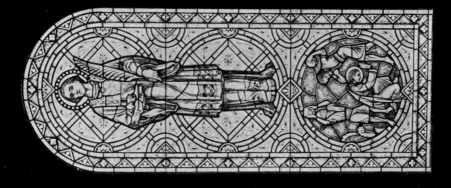

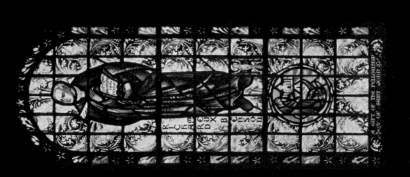

PLATE 14. LARGE FIGURES WITH BACKGROUND OF GRISAILLE OR FULL COLOR

PLATE 15.   CANOPY WINDOWS

PLATE 16.   CARTOONS FOR MODERN WINDOWS

Chapter 12

Middle Gothic Stained Glass:
The Fourteenth Century

IN THE EARLY GOTHIC PERIOD, MOST WINDOWS WERE LARGE SINGLE lights. The end of the thirteenth century saw a gradual development of the tracery windows which became a characteristic form in the fourteenth century.

At first, lancets were grouped in pairs under a rose light. Later, each lancet was subdivided into a pair of lights by stone mullions and tracery, which branched above into an elaborate mass of roses, quatrefoils, trefoils, and little openings of all shapes and sizes. These traceries often occupied half the space of an entire window. Figures were only introduced into the larger and more important divisions. Smaller ones contained heraldic symbols, heads of angels, demons, or saints. Less important openings were filled with grisaille or mere spots of color. With windows divided into comparatively narrow lights, the elaborate ironwork of the preceding period disappeared as its function was largely taken over by the stonework (see Plate 13, following p. 86).

Each long narrow light contained a border of alternate lengths of clear colored glass and white pieces, decorated with fleur-de-lis, castles, or small figures. These borders were outlined with a narrow band of white which separated them from the stonework.

The combination of figurework and grisaille, begun in the latter part of the thirteenth century, was further developed until large figures in colored glass, silhouetted against a background of grisaille became a distinct characteristic of this period (see Plate 14).

Grisaille windows were of trellis or quarry patterns between colored borders. Circles, lozenges, or straps in colored glass, with yellow (silver) stain added to the leaves in the painted design, gave them life and sparkle. Painting was delicate and took the form of straight, trailing, or coiled stems, with foliage recognizable as ivy, grape, maple, oak, etc. The bold black lines and crosshatched background of the thirteenth century were no longer used.

Patterns of realistic foliage were also scratched out or painted in black on grounds of colored glass. Popular forms of design were bunches of grapes, ivy leaves and berries, hyacinth blossoms, or a wavy ribbon leaf, like seaweed, with notched edges and a continuous median line. Foliage was deeply divided until it resembled a feather pattern. The Middle Gothic period is often referred to as the "Decorated period" because of these elaborate and realistic forms of design.

FIG. 34

Drawing in this period became more sentimental and less austere and objective than that of the previous centuries. There was an attempt to make figures appear graceful which resulted in affected gestures and an exaggerated swing of the hips. Drapery and human features were made more realistic by the use of stippling (paint daubed on with the bristle end of the brush). This gave a softening effect to hard lines and produced a more translucent tint than was possible with the smear formerly used.

Canopies over single figures became larger and larger, and were usually colored with silver stain. In mullioned windows where smaller figures stand under canopies, one above the other, the canopies form bands of brassy yellow across the whole window. Architectural details

[88]

in these canopies are flat in treatment with the crockets deeply cut like cypress foliage. No attempt was made to show perspective until the end of the century. Spaces above and below the canopies were filled with quarries or a trellis pattern in grisaille.

FIG. 35   Blessed James of Ulm

Medallion windows were enclosed by narrow colored borders of naturalistic foliage. The medallions were usually longer than broad, and arranged to form bands of color across the window divisions the same as canopies and figures. Backgrounds were usually of grisaille.

Jesse windows of the Middle Gothic period were less formal than

[89]

those of the Early Gothic. The genealogical tree took the definite form of a vine, but with leaves and grapes out of proportion to the small figures among its branches. Sometimes the figures were arranged in elongated medallions formed by the stems of the tree.

Silver stain was said to have been accidentally discovered in this century by the Blessed James of Ulm, Patron Saint of stained glass-men, when a silver button dropped from his coat and went into the kiln with a piece of glass. The silver-tin alloy of the button stained the glass a beautiful transparent yellow. However, it is known that more than a century before, silver stain had been used effectively in the Peter de Dane window found in York, England, dated about 1308. Blessed James of Ulm died in 1491 (Bib. 8) (Fig. 35, p. 89).

The yellow of silver stain penetrates into the glass itself and is absolutely permanent. It is dark or pale and ranges from greenish to orange, according to its strength and the heat of the fire. The color is always pure and bright but its metallic quality differs from pot metal yellow so that one can usually distinguish between them. The use of silver stain made it possible to show white and yellow on the same piece of glass without the use of separating leads. This combination was very popular for heraldic designs, crowns, and embroidery. The glass painter used yellow stain upon glass much as a gilder would use gold leaf on wood or stone, to give added brilliance to the points of interest. This made his windows very bright and gay (Bib. 5).

Olive or mossy green glass became popular for backgrounds instead of the usual blue or ruby. Flesh tints were paler and pinker, and white glass was more nearly white. Tawny brown and violet were added to the glassman's palette. Toward the end of the century paler and flatter tints of all colors were made. It was also possible to make glass in larger pieces, which made for a more patchy effect and less variety and balance of color.

Heraldry became quite the fashion and heraldic symbols or portraits of donors were introduced into the lower part of the windows and in the tracery lights. The fervent and devout religious spirit of the early glassmen was replaced by a more materialistic attitude. There was much catering to wealthy donors and short cuts were used in glazing to save time and money. This was made necessary, no doubt, by the economic effects of the Hundred Years' War and the Black Death which swept Europe and brought poverty and suffering to the glassmen as well as to thousands of others.

FIG. 36   Heraldic Charges

The chief characteristics of the Middle Gothic period may be summarized as follows (Bib. 13):

1. The grouping of two or more lights under one drip stone, subdivided by stone mullions and tracery
2. The simplification of the ironwork
3. The combination of figurework and grisaille
4. The use of natural plant forms in ornament
5. The use of painted diaper pattern on colored backgrounds
6. The style of drawing figures in an affected attitude like an elongated S
7. The extraordinary development of the canopy
8. The invention and use of silver stain
9. The quality of the glass and the colors

Late Gothic Glass: The Fifteenth Century

THE LATE GOTHIC PERIOD OF THE FIFTEENTH CENTURY WAS ALSO called the "Perpendicular period," especially in England. The development of the Perpendicular style of architecture called for tall narrow windows.

Windows in this period were still mosaic in character, but fewer leads were used. Glass could now be made in somewhat larger pieces.

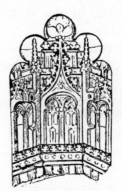

FIG. 37

More attention was given to painting than to glazing. "The glassman was no longer a glazier, thinking how he could carry his design further by the aid of paint, but a painter, thinking how by the aid of glazing he could get color into his design" (Bib. 5). Now for the first time he began to avoid as much as possible the use of leads, which he regarded as a blemish upon the glass.

The typical form of a Late Gothic design is a canopy window. The canopy is almost entirely in white glass and no longer a part of the picture but planned to enclose and frame the figures. The design varied in different parts of Europe but the work of one particular school was apt to be much of the same pattern. In England the canopies were of an architectural motif, patterned after the tabernacle-work in stone. In France and Germany the flamboyant canopy was popular. In some places a hint of hard times can be seen in the use of a standardized canopy as a means of saving money.

Figures stood on bases of tiled floor variations, under which were bands of archways, or single niches. Within these were illustrated, in small figures, scenes from the life of the persons represented above (see Plate 15). Large figures were usually shown draped in white or light tints against a background of rich color. Backgrounds for figures were often of brocaded drapery, hung from a rod on rings. Patterns in the drapery were of a conventional rosette design or like those found in woven materials from Italy or the Orient.

These elaborate ornamental details were made possible by the use of abrasion. This was a process, discovered in this century, of grinding away the colored layer in flashed glass, leaving the white. It was first done with red flash and later with blue, green, and other colors, making it possible to combine white and colored glass in one piece without the use of dividing leads. By the application of silver stain, yellow could also be introduced. With a single piece of blue flash glass it was thus possible to have blue, white, yellow, and green (made by the yellow stain on the blue) all in one piece.

Toward the end of the century, jewels were inserted in pieces of glass by drilling holes with the engraver's wheel. They were also applied to the surface with a vitreous paste which melted in the fire. Because the glass in the jewels was not the same consistency as that to which they were fastened, unequal shrinkage and expansion in varying temperatures caused them, in time, to work free from their setting.

Drawing in this period, done on paper or parchment instead of whitened boards, was dainty and realistic. French glassmen excelled in landscape backgrounds delicately painted on gray-blue glass. Silver stain applied to the light blue sky, introduced green for trees and bushes. Dark hills were glazed in purple against the blue sky and the horizon line was broken by quaint roofs and towers of buildings, or tree trunks in the foreground. Where the background was an interior scene, bits of the out-of-doors were shown through the archways.

Realism in figures was more advanced than in ornamental and land-scape design. Faces and hands, always of white glass, were delicately modeled by the process of stippling and the use of highlights and fine lines around the nose and eyes. Realistic portraits of donors were very much in evidence. Painting on glass, particularly in France, was an attempt to imitate the work of Flemish painters. The glassman relied for quality less on the glass itself than on what he painted upon it.

Colored glass in the deep rich tones of Early and Middle Gothic periods continued to be used, although it was always combined with a great deal of white. White glass, so characteristic of this period, was silvery white with a blue-green cast. Red glass was more scarlet and less ruby-like in color. Blue was lighter and more gray in tint; purple was no longer brownish but ranged to violet and lilac in the lighter shades. A peculiar rose-pink was made by the use of gold. A great variety of tints was secured by coating or flashing one color on another, as ruby on blue to produce purple.

After 1400, grisaille windows of the trellis pattern were no longer used. White backgrounds were divided into diamond shapes or quarries. In each quarry an individual design was painted, consisting of rosettes, formal motives, heraldic crests, emblems, or grotesque figures of animals or birds (see Fig. 38, p. 95).

Medallions in full color were only used occasionally, but roundels made of a single piece of glass, delicately painted in black and silver stain, became popular.

The best work of the fifteenth century was done in England during the first half of the century, and in France in the latter part. In England where the wool trade was bringing much money into the country, the glass craft guilds were powerful and exclusive. Their members were often prominent men like Sir John Petty, Thomas—sometimes called the "Glazier of Oxford," and Henry Smart who was a member of Parliament. York Minster contains outstanding examples of this period. Through a fortunate arrangement with one of Cromwell's leaders these treasures in glass were spared the destruction of the reformers. In France during the last half of the century, the drawing was better than in England and there was more variety in color schemes.

FIG. 38   Quarry Patterns

General characteristics of the fifteenth century or Late Gothic period are as follows (Bib. 13):

1. Type of canopy used
2. The increased use of white glass
3. Increased skill in the use of silver stain
4. A more advanced style of drawing with a delicate shading of faces and hands that was more like etching than painting
5. The use of decorative ornament in place of natural forms
6. The use of quarry windows in place of ornamental grisaille

Chapter 14

Post Gothic Period: The Sixteenth to Nineteenth Centuries

THE POST-GOTHIC PERIOD IN STAINED GLASS INCLUDES THE EARLY Renaissance of the sixteenth century, the Later Renaissance of the seventeenth century, and the Decadent Era of the eighteenth and nineteenth centuries.

The Early Renaissance period overlapped the Late Gothic. Whether a window happened to be in one style or the other depended more upon where it was designed than when it was made. Older and more conservative men clung to the way of their youth, while glassmen of the new generation attempted to imitate as nearly as possible the work of painters in oil. "They left their own region of poetic splendor in jewelled design and joined the painters of pictures . . . but the limitations of their media made them cringing apologists. They seemed to say, by implication, 'Please excuse us, but we must use an occasional lead line. It is too bad we cannot copy exactly the soft tones and melting colors of . . . the painter on canvas. Bear with us and we will do our best to please you under our unfortunate handicap of crude lead lines, bar lines, and light' " (Bib. 3).

In spite of this attitude the glazier could not be ignored. The artist seems to have designed his pictures with little or no consideration of the lead lines, and then left it up to the glazier to lead up as he pleased, usually in rectangular panes of convenient size. It was no longer necessary to cut and lead together separate pieces of glass for each color. The use of enamel made it possible to apply several colors to one large section of clear glass.

Enamel, which is pigment made by grinding colored glass and mixing it with a suitable vehicle, was applied to the surface of the glass. This vitreous compound was fused on the glass in the kiln, but

[97]

it did not penetrate it; and even when firmly attached, it was not permanently secure. Unable to withstand exposure to the weather, a great part of the enamel painting in windows of this period has flaked off. It is said that the window in New College Chapel, Oxford, by Sir Joshua Reynolds, (1780), considered to be the greatest example of painting on glass, has to be repainted about every twenty years.

The brown or black pigment used by glassmen from the first, to define form and control the light, was in reality enamel. However, the earliest enamel used to give actual color to glass was an iron red pigment discovered by a French artist, Jean Cousin, in 1525. It was used for lips and cheeks, and at first was applied as a tint on the back of the glass. Later, blue enamel was used on white glass to give delicate gradations of tint in the skies. Eventually other enamels were developed and applied to glass much as a painter in oils applies his pigment to canvas. Pieces of pot metal were still used where deep rich color was desired, but enamel was often applied to the pot metal to give depth to shadows. Lewis Day, in his *Stained Glass* states that, "No color applied to the surface of glass can have the limpid depth and luminosity of color suspended, as it were, within the glass itself. . . . To deepen the color of glass by painting upon it is to dull it" (Bib. 5). "Enamel color compared with pot metal is poor, thin and garish. Painted shadow is heavy, and lacks the translucency of glass and the transparency of shadow" (Bib. 4). When the glass painter ceased to get light into shadows, all the glory was gone.

The pictorial treatment of glass was fully developed in the Later Renaissance period of the seventeenth century. Glass was designed not as a window, but rather as an illuminated picture to be seen through a window opening. They sacrificed that decorative quality so easily obtained by using pot metal and lead lines, for the realistic effect of an oil painting. The strong glazing lines, still necessary, did not combine well with the delicate painting, but made the painting appear weak by comparison. Architecture was drawn in correct perspective, figures were portrayed with all the realism of light and shade, and in landscape attempts were even made to show atmospheric effects.

According to one authority, "The seventeenth and eighteenth centuries were a period of complete decadence in the craft, when translucence was sacrificed to painting, and the picture became more

[98]

obvious than the glass" (Bib. 21). It should not be said that all stained glass of this period was bad. The Renaissance glass painters did something in their own way—which is the right of all artists. We shall not attempt to describe here the various types of Renaissance glass because they are not suitable for adaptation by the Frengosi method. For further information on this period consult the bibliography.

The Reformation curtailed the manufacture of stained glass. It was prohibited for church use by the Puritans. The little that was made was used in heraldic charges which began to appear in private homes and public buildings. During the Reformation, zealous reformers who considered all forms of symbolism in the church as idolatrous, were responsible for the destruction of untold quantities of artistic treasures in carved wood and stone, and masterpieces on canvas or in stained glass.

Richard Culmer, placed in charge of Canterbury Cathedral under the Commonwealth, and known to his enemies as "Blue Dick," relates with glee how he stood on a ladder sixty steps high with a long pole in his hand and "rattled down proud Beckett's glassy bones" (Bib. 13). In some old English records it is stated that the amount of glass removed from a single cathedral was so large that cartloads of it were used to fill in marshy ground and ditches. Beautiful sculptured stone from ruined churches was used to form foundations for new roads built across swampy ground. Accounts are given of stone sold at sixpence a load and used for stables in which one may still find fragments of window tracery and delicately wrought ecclesiastical symbols. Hitching posts were often made from beautifully carved capitals. One writer says that entire shiploads of ancient illuminated manuscripts were sent to the continent from England and sold for common wrapping paper, or given to the peasants to light their kitchen fires (Bib. 47).

Churches were stripped of all beauty, for symbols of any kind were considered as idols, and the idea was abroad that beauty of spirit and beauty of expression were opposed to each other. Mr. Frank Wilson in his *Outline of Christian Symbolism*, says: "The reformers could not abolish symbolism; they simply substituted the long coat for the long vestment, and the hard bench for the kneeling stool. Even the Quakers kept silence as a symbol of their contempt of symbolism" (Bib. 49).

[99]

SIMULATED STAINED GLASS

The nineteenth century brought, especially in England, a revival of the Gothic form in church architecture which encouraged a return to medieval techniques in glass painting. Most critics agree that windows made in this period were slavish copies of old windows, made with modern glass in all its flawlessness. This smooth clear glass lacked the luminous qualities of ancient glass with its many imperfections. There seems to have been little understanding of the problems and feelings of the medieval craftsmen, which make it easy to distinguish between the old and the new.

Chapter 15

Stained Glass in America

TOWARD THE END OF THE NINETEENTH CENTURY AN INTERESTING development took place in the stained glass craft in America. Mr. John La Farge, a well-known artist, assisted by a talented glassmaker in Philadelphia, after extensive experiments succeeded in producing a type of glass known as "Opalescent." It was made in large sheets of varying texture and beautiful shades with striations and masses of opaque white glass having the appearance of "Opal." At first these sheets were either gradations of one color, or a simple combination of red and yellow, or violet and green. Later they were produced with varied markings, tints, and textures that made them easily adapted to natural forms. The only parts in windows made from this glass that required painting and firing were the faces, feet, and hands of the figures. All other parts of the design were selected and cut from the variegated sheets so that the shading or color form within the glass gave the desired pictorial effect.

La Farge and Frederick Wilson, an equally talented artist for many years with the Tiffany studio, produced many wonderful color effects with opalescent glass. The colors were soft, delicate, and clean, in contrast to other windows of that day in which the colors were "dirtied" by heavy matts of black paint used to subdue the garishness of the glass imported from Europe at that time. These men were painters, trained in the realistic school. In their desire to secure pictorial effects of light and shade, they often plated one piece of colored glass over another, and in so doing they lost sight of the most charming quality of antique glass, its active translucence.

Mr. Connick in *Adventures in Light and Color* explains how the difference in the effect of opalescent glass and that of translucent pot metal can be shown by the following experiment. "Take a small piece of waxed or tracing paper and hold it to the light. It represents the opacity of opalescent glass. Punch it full of holes with a pin or knife point and you have at once an active translucence that brings your piece of paper alive. . . . That bit of paper full of holes, represents the translucence of ancient glass; the quality that was almost lost in later painted glass, and entirely lost in opalescent picture windows" (Bib. 3).

This loss of translucence gave rise, no doubt, to the popular legend that the art of medieval stained glass is a lost one. This lost art legend is quite easy to believe when one sees the atrocious pink-yellow-violet windows in many of our American churches, which are the products of those men of lesser talent who tried to imitate the works of Wilson and La Farge.

American Art-Glass

"At the time opalescent glass was introduced to the craft, there grew up a host of commercial glass firms in England, Germany, and America. These firms, organized and run on a factory basis, flooded the world, and especially the United States, with some of the most unfortunate creations that have ever masqueraded under the name of art" (Bib. 21). These wares were known in this country as "American art-glass."

Most of us have grown up in churches built during the heyday of this American art-glass era. The sweetly sentimental picture-windows of our time represent a low point in the decadence of the art which began as far back as the fifteenth century. The commercialization of art-glass made art safe for moneymakers. Skillful workmen produced sheets of marbleized glass which was turned out by the yard like linoleum. These ornamental concoctions resembled foliage, ground, skies, or water, backs of sheep, flesh, or flowers, and foldlike ridges known as "drapery glass." The more clever the glassmaker, the less talent was required to arrange sections of this glass into a complete picture window.

"Units of art-glass were turned out in quantities with no more aesthetic worries than had the manufacturers of paper boxes" (Bib. 3). Energetic salesmen peddled pretty arrangements of "Good Shepherds" and sweet girl angels or "Boys-in-Temple" whose faces resembled photographs furnished by loving donors. Lilies, palms, crosses, and crowns were intertwined with frilly scrolls executed in bilious shades of pink, yellow, and lavender. Life-size figures often resembled "curious bearded Bavarian peasants who might easily be mistaken for House of David baseball players, with their feet resting airily on pink thunder heads" (Bib. 48).

Products of this period are "mawkishly pretty or frankly horrid, as the fates assigned" (Bib. 3). The pernicious influence of these dull and ugly things on sensitive spirits is hard to estimate. One clergyman has said, "A stained glass window is glorious when it is good, but it is the Devil's own advocate when it is bad." There are churches where it is difficult for one to lift his heart in an attitude of worship because of the dreadful color combinations found in the windows.

During the early part of the twentieth century the revolutionary influence of two eminent architects, Ralph Adams Cram and Bertram Grosvenor Goodhue, brought about in America a revival of the Gothic style in architecture. Other architects had begun to turn to the Gothic form for a solution to the many new problems presented by the development of the skyscraper; but these men, long associated in the firm of Cram, Goodhue, and Ferguson, directed most of their efforts toward ecclesiastical buildings. Their work was considered superlative from the very beginning (Bib. 37).

Mr. Cram is the author of several books. In his first, *Church Architecture*, he heaps scorn on the cater-cornered auditoriums, bow-shaped floors, and crude decorations in church buildings of the late nineteenth century. He succeeded in impressing clergymen and laymen with the fact that, "A church which willfully or carelessly declines the gentle aid that Art can lend, fights a battle against almost hopeless odds" (Bib. 37). Tallmadge, in his *Story of Architecture in America*, says: "The church awaited a new gospel of beauty; and so when these two knights (Cram and Goodhue) . . . charged the cohorts of ugliness and sham, a paean of thanksgiving for deliverance ascended from every parish" (Bib. 37).

Ralph Adams Cram gathered about him in his work a number of American stained glass artists who exploded once and for all the popular legend that the art of medieval stained glass is a lost art. Their works are conclusive proof that ancient color formulas and processes may have been lost or disregarded in the past, but they have also been rediscovered by modern chemists and glassmakers. These artists did not attempt to reproduce the windows of the Middle Ages. That is not possible. Old windows have the magic charm of antiquity of an ancient Persian rug which has been softened and mellowed by time. However, these leading glassmen, many of whom are contemporary, have given much time to the study of ancient windows. They have rediscovered the principles and rules which governed the medieval craftsmen. By putting these rules to work within the limitations of transparent glass and lead, they are now producing in England and America, church buildings with windows expressive of the life and spirit of our time. Windows from our finest American studios are comparable to the medieval masterpieces of the Gothic periods.

Few people in America are ever privileged to see the ancient cathedral windows of France and England. Others are able only occasionally to visit the great Gothic churches in our own land, and see the masterpieces of contemporary artists. Some people are fortunate enough to worship regularly in churches that contain windows representative of the best in stained glass. However, in many churches where fine Gothic windows have been installed beside the opalescent picture type so popular in the last century, there are those who prefer the latter because they are more familiar and realistic. The unique beauty of clear vibrating color-in-glass is not understood or fully appreciated.

The average person today is not aware of what is good or bad in stained glass. One reason for this is that stained glass is a subject that does not lend itself to the familiar forms of advertising or popular presentation. Stained glass is difficult to describe by means of the printed page, for the very thing that makes a good window unique cannot be captured by printer's ink on paper. The usual reproductions in black and white are about as adequate in describing a window as are anatomical charts for living creatures, or maps for the living beauty of land or sea. Even the finest color photograph gives only a hint of the appearance of the window at the moment the film was exposed. In order to record a satisfactory impression of a stained glass window it would be necessary to have a series of color photographs taken at various hours of the day in varying weather and in different seasons of the year.

[104]

Music recorded in black and white by means of notes and staffs must be translated into sound before it can be enjoyed. Just so, stained glass must be seen under the transforming influence of the sun before it can be fully appreciated and understood.

Appreciation and understanding of this significant form of beauty must be developed, just as in other expressions of art. We go to great trouble to acquaint our children with the best in painting and music. Good books and fine reproductions of great masters of the brush and baton are found in all homes of education and culture. But the modern child's contact with color-in-glass is usually limited to company dishes and beverage bottles of many varieties.

Young people in medieval times were thoroughly familiar with the windows of their cathedral, as evidenced by a passage in an old catechism of the Diocese of Triquier that asks, "What should one do upon entering a Cathedral?" The answer reads, "Take holy water, adore the Blessed Sacrament, then walk all around the edifice and look at the stained glass" (Bib. 1).

Children who today attend churches where there are fine windows ought to be as familiar with their story and particular form of beauty as they are with the best works in their libraries or albums of symphonic recordings. Many such churches have prepared illustrated brochures to assist parishioners and visitors in understanding the stories and symbols found in their windows.

All the halftone illustrations in this book are reproductions of contemporary works of American studios in various parts of the United States. They do not necessarily represent the best work of each studio but have been chosen with the consent and through the courtesy of the artists because of their appropriateness to the text and purpose of this publication.

"America lags behind in many of the arts, but in the matter of stained glass it is doubtful whether any other country of the present day has produced more of it, or as many truly worthy examples" (Bib. 48).

Appendix

1. MATERIALS AND SUPPLIES
2. REPORT ON FRENGOSI PROJECTS
   A. Medallions for Christmas Gifts.
   B. A worship center for the church school.
   C. Kaleidoscopes containing stained glass.
   D. Stained glass shade-pulls.
3. WHERE TO SEE REPRESENTATIVE EXAMPLES OF FINE STAINED GLASS IN THE UNITED STATES
4. GLOSSARY
5. BIBLIOGRAPHY, ANNOTATED
6. NOTES ON PLATES
7. NOTES ON FIGURES

1. List of Materials Needed

I. FOR THE SMALL COLORED PRELIMINARY SKETCH, DRAWN TO SCALE
1. White water color paper
2. Medium hard pencil, #2
3. Ruler
4. India Ink—black
5. Drawing pen
6. Water colors and suitable brush

II. FOR THE FULL-SIZED CARTOON
1. White or brown wrapping paper (light weight). Small sheets can be pieced together if necessary
2. Ruler or yardstick, T square, and triangle
3. Charcoal or soft pencil. Charcoal pencils are very convenient and come hard, soft, and very soft
4. Black ink (diluted) or gray tempora paint for making all lead lines and crossbars gray
5. Black ink or paint for indicating on the cartoon all lines and patterns which define the form and control the light

III. FOR THE BLACK STENCIL TO SIMULATE LEAD
1. Black building or sheathing paper. This can be purchased by the roll from any builder's supply company. Other black papers are usable but are apt to be stiff and tough, making it difficult to cut or glue securely to the textured glass. Black sheathing paper is flexible and very easy to cut. Its thickness and surface texture make it very suitable for simulating the leads and ironwork in a stained glass window or medallion
2. White or yellow carbon paper, sold in stationery stores, for transferring the lead lines in the cartoon to the black paper
3. Sharp knife, razor blade cutter, or pointed scissors
4. Glue—Le Page's Double Strength or McCormick's Iron Glue

IV. GLASS
1. Velvex—plain. Catalogue #7132. Manufactured by the Blue Ridge Glass Co. and marketed by Libby-Owens-Ford Co. It can be purchased from any glass dealer who carries their products
2. English Double Rolled glass has a texture similar to Velvex and

can be substituted if Velvex is not available. It is carried by all dealers in stained glass or can be ordered through a local stained glass studio

3. Scrap pieces of stained glass to be used as points of reference or in making stained glass kaleidoscopes. These can be obtained from a local stained glass studio or from the author for 50 cents per lb.

V. PAINTS

1. Oil paints in tubes—any reliable brand
   a. Harrison red
   b. Yellow ocher
   c. Ultramarine blue
   d. Phthalocyanine blue. In some brands this is known as "Thalo" blue or "Monastral" blue
   e. Phthalocyanine green—also called "Thalo" or "Monastral"
   f. Burnt umber
   g. Lampblack

   These colors are known to be sunfast and are comparable to the colors used by medieval craftsmen in stained glass

2. Prang Dek-All colors—a product of the American Crayon Co. These newly developed paints appeared on the market as this book went to press. They offer some advantages over oil paints in that they are more translucent and will not flake or crack off the glass in time. Dek-All is now sold in sets of six colors: red, yellow, blue, green, black, and white. As in all new products, changes and improvements will be made from time to time. Additional colors will be offered and made available in the single jar as well as in sets. For further information concerning the use of Dek-All with the Frengosi method of simulating stained glass, address the American Crayon Co. or the author

VI. BRUSHES

1. #7 bristle or #11 flat red sable for applying the color
2. #2 red sable (pointed) for painting with black to define the form and control the light

VII. MISCELLANEOUS

1. Turpentine for diluting paint and cleaning brushes used with either oil paint or Dek-All
2. Soft cleansing tissue for removing or stippling oil paint
3. Soft cloths for wiping brushes

APPENDIX

4. Toothpicks and a small amount of cotton to make tiny applicators for removing paint
5. Clear Valspar or silk screen varnish for the protective coating on glass colored with oil paint. Not needed for Dek-All
6. Wire coat hangers for making a rack to hold glass up against the light
7. Black passe partout tape, sold in stationery stores, for binding the edges of a medallion
8. Lead came for binding the edges of a medallion. Came comes in various widths. The 3/8th or 1/2 inch are best for binding the edges of a medallion. Lead cames are sold by the box, but arrangements can be made through local stained glass studios to purchase a few strips at a time
9. Solder and soldering iron for soldering corners of lead binding
10. Picture wire for hanging medallions

[111]

2. Report on Frengosi Projects

Simulating stained glass by the Frengosi method has been given a thorough laboratory test in the church school of the First Presbyterian Church of Englewood, N.J.

The Junior Department of this school was transferred for assembly and worship from the large Sunday school room to the Ladies' Parlor. This room has an open fireplace and is beautifully furnished with large davenports, overstuffed chairs, a grand piano, attractive lamps, and several tables. The first problem facing the director of the department was how to create an atmosphere of worship in living-room surroundings.

The only way to place enough straight chairs to accommodate the group in the room was to have them face either the fireplace and a door through which everyone entered, or the large bay window in the east wall. Because of the interruptions bound to occur due to late-comers, it was decided to have the chairs face the bay window. The problem then was how to eliminate the glare of the morning sun and cut off the view of the driveway and entrance to another wing of the building. Plans were made to fix up the bay as a miniature chancel and cover the windows with portable panels of wallboard and simulated stained glass to be made by the children. The drapes on either side of the bay were drawn across the windows until the panels were made.

For several Sundays the theme of the worship services was "Beauty in God's House." The subject of Christian symbols in stained glass was introduced by presenting some of the material given in chapters 10 and 11. Colorful pieces of scrap stained glass and sample Frengosi medallions were exhibited and a special offering box, appropriately decorated, was passed each week to receive extra gifts to cover the cost of the proposed windows. A kaleidoscope that makes stained glass window designs was demonstrated and all those who wished to make one were invited to remain for an extended session during the church hour (see directions on p. 115).

A. Medallions Made for Christmas Gifts

After creating an interest in stained glass through the making of the kaleidoscopes, those who wanted to make a Fregosi medallion were asked

[112]

to come Saturday mornings from 10 to 12 o'clock. A choice of two mimeographed patterns was offered. All the materials were furnished by the school. The children paid 25 cents to cover the cost of each piece of glass used. Most of them transferred the pattern to the black paper and did the cutting at home. The cut-out black stencil was brought to the Saturday class between the pages of an old magazine. This stencil was then glued to the glass and the painting done at small tables pushed close to the windows. As many as 12 children were able to work at one time.

Before choosing the colors for their medallions they were taken on a conducted tour to see the various stained glass windows in the church building. The painting was done in one or two sessions. The varnish was applied the next week and while it was drying most of the boys and girls started a second medallion. The black lines were added the following week, making it possible to complete a medallion in three or four two-hour sessions—with time out for a recess at the end of an hour.

The Sunday before Christmas all the finished medallions were hung in the windows of the east room as the Ladies' Parlor is called. A large medallion of real stained glass was borrowed from the August Stained Glass Studio, Paramus, N.J., and hung in the center of one of the large leaded windows. The small medallions made by the children, which by prearrangement were the same size as the sections in the leaded window, were grouped around the large medallion. Small pieces of scrap stained glass were bound on the edges with black friction tape and fastened here and there in the corners of the leaded sections of the window to help balance the colors and tie the whole thing together. The effect was similar to Plate 2, following p. 30, and many adults who saw it thought it was a new installation of stained glass.

After Christmas there were some requests from parents for duplicate medallions, but most of the children were eager to begin work on the large windows for the worship center.

B. A WORSHIP CENTER FOR THE CHURCH SCHOOL

A carpenter was engaged to construct wooden frames that would fit snugly inside the stone framework of each of the four leaded windows of the large bay. These frames were covered with sheets of Upson board. An opening was cut in the center of each panel into which the Frengosi glass could be inserted. This opening was arranged so that nine sections of the leaded window were exposed. Picture molding was used around the opening to hold the glass in place. A small hole was drilled into the cement seam of the stonework on each side of the four windows and small slide bolts fastened opposite them on the wooden frame. Two bolts were enough to hold each panel firmly in place against the window (see Frontispiece and Plate 3b, following p. 30). The panels were painted a soft light green to match the large pottery lamps in the room, and to harmonize with the dark green upholstery of some of the chairs. The backs of the panels, seen from the street, were painted a light tan to match the lining of the drapes at the other windows.

A small colored sketch was made of one complete panel and each of the four glass medallions. The border design is a conventionalized grapevine and in each corner is a Christian symbol appropriate to the subject portrayed in the glass medallion. Down the center of each panel is a wide decorative band containing other selected symbols. As soon as the panels were made by the carpenter they were used on Sunday mornings. There was keen interest in the progress of the decoration from week to week. When a new symbol was added the child who cut it out or painted it was allowed to explain its meaning to the group.

The border design was divided into two units and mimeographed patterns were made of them and of each of the symbols. These patterns were stapled to a piece of black building paper of the same size and a smaller piece of white carbon paper provided with each set. These were given out on Sunday morning to be cut out at home. The Cub Scouts assisted in the cutting out of some of the designs, and of the 148 units cut by more than thirty different children, only 2 had to be rejected because of careless workmanship.

The black stencil-like units of the design were glued to the green Upson board panels and the spaces between the lines colored with water color poster paint. The colors in the border were gold, brown, and green to harmonize with the colors of the drapes and furniture, with spots of red and blue for the grapes and touches of red in the symbols.

The cartoons for the glass medallions were made by the author, and were all adaptations of designs by well-known glassmen. They had to be adapted to the simulated iron bars which were made to coincide with the lead mullions in the large window. She also transferred the design to the black paper and cut it out, but only in order to save time. Several of the children were capable of doing the cutting but time was short and they were anxious to complete the project for Easter Sunday.

Painting the glass was done right in the window for which it was designed. The sheet of glass was supported in the window by means of a table-horse. Scrap pieces of stained glass were placed in the window as points of reference and the children took turns applying the color according to the colored sketch. About fifteen different youngsters painted on the border and the medallions. The angels shown in the frontispiece were painted by the eight-year-old sister of one of the junior girls.

The four panels and two center medallions were completed and dedicated on Easter Sunday. The curtains were drawn across the bay for the first part of the service. At a given signal they were parted, and just at that moment the sun, which had not shown itself for three days, flooded the room and splashed colored rays of light across the altar and the chancel carpet. The top of the altar is the cover of the long radiator under the two center windows. The face of the altar is made from an old door found in the church basement. It was cut off a little at one end and sanded and varnished by one of the boys' classes with the help of their teacher. A special offering was received at another time to provide a suitable altar cloth and frontal for the reading stand, which was made from a discarded radio cabinet.

A brief statement of the meaning of each symbol was printed on the dedication program. The solo, sung by a senior girl, mentioned the birds and flowers and creatures of the field pictured in the glass medallions.

This worship center is set up each week in just a few minutes with a minimum of effort. It adds much to the beauty and dignity of the worship service. The project has created a new interest in stained glass and Christian symbols not only among the boys and girls but also among parents and other adults who are often brought into the room to admire a particular bird, flower, or figure that a child has painted.

C. KALEIDOSCOPES CONTAINING STAINED GLASS

For demonstration purposes a kaleidoscope about 9 inches long and 2 inches in diameter was purchased at a toy counter for 69 cents. The small beads and bits of colored glass and the frosted glass disk in the cap end of the instrument were removed. The frosted glass disk was replaced with a transparent disk cut from a piece of heavyweight cellophane or old cleaned photograph film.

Small scraps of stained glass, varying in size from 1/2 to 1 square inch were selected and placed on a piece of black paper. A line was drawn around each piece of glass and the resulting pattern cut out of the black paper. The center of each pattern was then cut out leaving a narrow black border or frame which was glued on the corresponding piece of glass. Designs were painted in black on some of the pieces, particularly the red, and when the glue and paint were dry these pieces were placed in the

[115]

cap end of the kaleidoscope. The designs thus formed are suitable for stained glass because each color is outlined and separated from the others by black.

A homemade kaleidoscope can be made from a round oatmeal box and two pieces of window glass:

1. Remove the top or cover from an oatmeal box
2. Line the inside of the box with a piece of black paper. This makes it unnecessary to use mirrors
3. Cut a round hole ½ inch in diameter in the bottom of the box about ¼ inch from the edge
4. Cut two strips of window glass about 3½ inches wide and the same length as the box without the cover. Hinge these two pieces of glass together along the long side with a piece of black passe partout tape. Place the pieces inside the box with the hinge directly under the small hole in the bottom of the box. Look into the box from the top toward the hole in the bottom and adjust the angle of the two pieces of glass until the round spot of light coming through the hole is reflected an equal number of times. Be sure each reflection is a complete circle. A 45° angle will produce eight reflections and make an eight-sided unit of design. A 60° angle will produce six reflections and the design units will be six sided, etc. The pieces of glass can be fastened in place at the desired angle by means of cardboard or wooden supports taped to the lining of the box
5. Cut out the center of the round cover of the oatmeal box, leaving a ½ inch border or rim around the edge
6. Cut a strip of bristol board or single face corrugated board, 2 inches wide and a little longer than the circumference of the box cover
7. Fasten this strip, by sewing rather than gluing, to that part of the lid which laps over the end of the box. This overlap on a Quaker or Mother's Oats box is very narrow and needs to be extended so the cover or cap can be turned on the box without working it off the end. Overlap the ends of this strip and sew them together down the 2-inch side
8. Cut two round disks of heavyweight cellophane or old, cleaned photograph film to fit inside the cover of the box. The ½-inch rim around the edge will keep them from falling out
9. Prepare several pieces of scrap stained glass as described above, and place them in the cover on top of the cellophane disk

10. Cover the pieces of glass with the second disk and place the cover on the end of the box

11. Hold the box toward the light and look into it through the small hole in the bottom. The designs formed by the reflection of the colors in the box will vary according to the angle of the reflectors and the arrangement of the various colors. By turning the cover on the end of the box, the pieces of glass will shift position and a new design will be formed

12. Combinations of color can be varied by changing the size and color of the pieces of stained glass in the kaleidoscope

D. Stained Glass Shade-Pulls

A scrap piece of stained glass makes a colorful ornament for the end of a shade cord.

1. Select a piece of stained glass and frame it with $\frac{3}{16}$-inch came.

2. Solder a wire loop to the came at the top and slipknot the shade cord through it, as in Figure 39A

Several pieces can be fitted together with lead came and then framed (see Fig. 39B). Patterns in black paint can also be added, as in C.

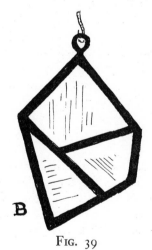

A B C

Fig. 39

3. WHERE TO SEE REPRESENTATIVE EXAMPLES OF FINE STAINED GLASS IN THE UNITED STATES

A rather brief list appeared in *Liturgical Arts,* Vol. 6, Second Quarter, 1937, and a longer list is given in *Adventures in Light and Color* by Charles J. Connick.

The Stained Glass Association of America is now compiling, under the direction of their Chairman of Education and Publicity, a *Guide to Stained Glass in the United States.* All schools of thought are to be represented—antique, opalescent, traditional, and experimental. Classification will be by geographical areas, under state and city headings.

The manuscript for this *Guide* was submitted for approval at the 1948 convention of the Stained Glass Association of America, and should be available soon. Address inquiries to Mr. Fred Oppliger, General Secretary, Stained Glass Association of America, 822 Wilmington Ave., St. Louis, Mo.

4. GLOSSARY

ANNEALING: The process of slowly cooling glass after it has been fired in a kiln.

ANTIQUE GLASS: Glass which is made in imitation of the qualities of ancient glass.

CAMES: Strips of lead of various widths and 3 to 4 feet long that look like miniature steel girders, used to bind together the many pieces of glass in a stained glass window.

CANOPY: An architectural ornament suggesting a carved niche in which a figure is placed. It was common in all periods of medieval windows.

CARTOON: The full-size drawing of a window design on paper.

CROSSBAR: A horizontal iron bar fastened into the stone framework of a window to which sections of the stained glass window are fastened. These are also known as T bars.

DIAPER: An all-over pattern, which may be geometric or foliated, used for backgrounds in medallion windows, and made out of small pieces of glass or scratched out of black paint on colored glass with a sharp point.

FLUX: The solvent which assists in the melting of glass.

GLAZIER: One who does glazing.

GLAZING: The act of setting pieces of glass into lead came and soldering it on both sides at the joints, to bind the many pieces together within a frame.

GRISAILLE: From the French word *gris* meaning gray. A type of stained glass in which narrow bands of glass, usually colored and forming a geometrical design, are used against a background of white or light glass of various tints, upon which is painted designs in outline set off by crosshatching or slight shading.

KALEIDOSCOPE: An instrument containing small bits of colored glass, which by an arrangement of mirrors appear in a variety of beautiful patterns when turned around.

LANCET: Long narrow window opening with a pointed arch. These occur singly or grouped in a single window, with or without tracery.

MULLION: The vertical bars dividing a window into sections.

PATINA: The film produced on very old windows by the action of wind, rain, and driving dust. Patina can be produced artificially by the use of chemicals.

POT METAL: Glass that is stained or colored in the pot, while in a molten stage, by the addition of various metallic oxides.

QUARRIES: Small diamond, square, or other shaped panes of glass used in plain glazing.

ROSE WINDOW: A circular window divided into compartments by mullions or tracery radiating from the center and suggesting the petals of a flower.

STANCHION: A vertical iron bar set into the stone framework of a window to which sections of the stained glass are fastened for support.

TRACERY: The ornamental frames or divisions at the top of a Gothic window, and the openings formed thereby.

TRANSLUCENT: Allowing the passage of light but not of a clear view of any object beyond; semitransparent.

TRANSPARENT: Admitting the passage of light, and a clear view of objects beyond.

WHEEL WINDOW: An adaptation of the rose window with tracery in the form of spokes radiating from the center.

5. BIBLIOGRAPHY*

STAINED GLASS

1. Aubert, Marcel. *French Cathedral Windows of the Twelfth and Thirteenth Century*. New York, Oxford University Press, 1939. This book contains many colored illustrations of medieval master pieces in stained glass. The color plates are said to be some of the finest reproductions of stained glass ever made. $5.00

2. Bushnell, A. J. de Havilland. *Storied Windows*. New York, The Macmillan Company, 1914. A traveler's introduction to old French stained glass of the 12th to the 16th centuries, written from the view of the layman rather than that of the craftsman or designer.

3. Connick, Charles, J. *Adventures in Light and Color*. New York, Random House, Inc., 1937. This is considered to be the finest work written in English on the stained glass craft. It contains over 400 pages of text, more than 100 illustrations in black and white, and 40 color plates. It was published in two forms, one which sold for $12.50 and a de luxe edition for $25.00. At this time (1948) it is out of print but available in the Fine Arts Department of most public libraries. A new printing is contemplated. This book is inspiring and informative to the lay reader.

4. Day, Lewis F. *Windows—A Book About Stained and Painted Glass*. London, R. F. Batsford; New York, Charles Scribner's Sons, 1879. This is a large volume profusely illustrated with pen drawings and photo-tints. It is an excellent book of source material for the amateur designer of stained glass.

5. Day, Lewis F. *Stained Glass*. London, Chapman & Hall, Ltd., 1903. A handbook for the Victoria and Albert Museum, briefly tracing the historic development of the stained glass craft. The

* Nearly all books on stained glass are now out of print, but are available in most large public libraries.

illustrations are from the drawings and glass in the collection owned by the museum.

6. Eden, F. Sidney. *Ancient Stained and Painted Glass*. London, Cambridge University Press, 1933.
An interesting handbook of English and French styles.

7. *Encyclopedia Americana*. New York, Americana Corporation, 1948.
Pages 471 through 471h. contain an excellent article entitled Stained Glass, written by two outstanding members of the craft, Harold W. Rambusch and Henry Lee Willet. It is illustrated with many plates in black and white and color.

8. Holiday, Henry. *Stained Glass as an Art*. London, Macmillan and Company, Limited. New York, The Macmillan Company, 1896.
A book about the artistic possibilities of stained glass, written by a practical and successful artist in glass.

9. Knowles, John. *History of the York School of Glass Painting*. New York, The Macmillan Company, 1936.
This was also published serially in the Bulletin of the Stained Glass Association of America, beginning in 1929. It is well illustrated with many sketches and photographs of work by the author and deals with the characteristics of the York style and technique.

10. Rackham, Bernard. *A Guide to the Collection of Stained Glass*. Victoria and Albert Museum, London Board of Education, 1936.

11. Read, Herbert. *English Stained Glass*. New York, G. P. Putnam's Sons, 1926.
He traces the course of stained glass as a mode of aesthetic expression in relation to the history of art in general. Illustrated with black and white drawings and several collotypes in color.

12. Rogers, Frances and Beard, Alice. *500 Years of Glass*. New York, J. B. Lippincott Company, 1948.
A survey of the history of glass, full of anecdotes and human interest material on the craft of glass making. Chapter VII entitled "Pictorial Windows," gives a brief history of the development of stained glass windows.

13. Saint, Lawrence B. and Arnold, Hugh. *Stained Glass of the Middle Ages in England and France*. London, A. & C. Black, Ltd., 1913.

A readable study of typical windows of each century from the
12th to the 15th, with a brief outline of the history of stained
glass. Written by Hugh Arnold and illustrated with 50 excellent
reproductions of colored drawings by Lawrence B. Saint, who
made many of the windows in the Washington Cathedral,
Washington, D.C.

14. Theophilus. (also called Rugerus) *An Essay Upon the Various Arts.*
Translated by Robert Hendrie. London, John Murray, 1847.
A handbook of medieval craft work in three parts. The second
part is on glassmaking and stained glass. Copies of this manuscript have been found in various great libraries and museums
of Europe and England. Very little is known about Theophilus
himself but most authorities believe he lived in the 11th
century.

15. Viollet-le-Duc, E. *Dictionnaire Raisonne de l'Architecture Francaise.*
Paris, B. Bance, 1861. Ve A. Morel and Cie, 1879.
Until recent years this has been perhaps the only attempt to
outline and record the theories and rules of color, light, and
optics that apparently governed the medieval masters of the
craft. Most of its simple and intelligent formulas stand the
test of actual studio practice and are used today by the leading
stained glassmen of our time.

16. Viollet-le-Duc, E. *Vitrail. Stained Glass.*
A translation of the previous book by Leicester Holland in 1910,
in an edition of only 10 copies. It was reprinted as a serial in
Stained Glass, the bulletin of the Stained Glass Association of
America, 1931-1932.

17. Viollet-le-Duc, E. *Medieval Stained Glass.* Atlanta, Ga. The Lullwater
Press, 1947.
A translation of the same work by F. P. Smith in an edition of
500 copies.

18. Westlake, N. H. J. *A History of Design in Painted Glass.* London and
Oxford, James Parker & Co., 1881.
The work of a master craftsman and scholar, which has served
as the standard reference since its publication. 4 vols.

19. Whall, Christopher W. *Stained Glass Work.* New York, D. Appleton-
Century Company, Inc., 1905; reprinted London, Sir Isaac Pit-
man & Sons, Ltd., 1920.

[123]

APPENDIX

An excellent handbook on stained glass, written by a distinguished master craftsman and creative artist. He exerted a powerful influence as a teacher, and his students have contributed largely to the advancement of modern stained glass. The book contains many practical diagrams and line drawings, and a few reproductions of windows by the author and others.

20. Winston, Charles. *Memoirs Illustrative of the Art of Glass Painting*. London, John Murry, 1865.
    A collection of writings dealing with the stained glass of many English churches.

ARTICLES AND PAMPHLETS ON STAINED GLASS

21. Reynolds, J. G. *Stained Glass*. American Architect and the Architectural Review, Vol. CXXI Numbers 2394 to 2399.

22. Reynolds, J. G. *Stained Glass—Its Spiritual Significance*. Cathedral Age. Vol. XIX No. 4, 1944.
    A periodical published at Washington Cathedral in the Nation's Capital for the members of the National Cathedral Association.

23. *Stained Glass*.
    A quarterly devoted to the craft of stained and painted glass. Published by the Stained Glass Association of America, 37 Walden Street, Newtonville, Mass. $2.00 per year.

24. *The Story of Stained Glass*.
    A booklet prepared and sponsored by the Stained Glass Association of America. It contains a beautiful reproduction 5½ by 8¼ inches of "Our Lady of the Beautiful Window" in Chartres Cathedral; also many small line drawings illustrating the making of a stained glass window. There is, in addition, a brief bibliography and glossary. Available in quantity lots at 25¢ each. Address General Secretary, Mr. Fred P. Oppliger, 822 Wilmington Ave., St. Louis 11, Mo.

25. *A Guide to the Washington Cathedral*. Washington, D.C.
    Profusely illustrated with black and white and many colored reproductions of stained glass and other art treasures in the cathedral. Address National Cathedral Association, Washington Cathedral, Mount Saint Alban, Washington 16, D.C. 75¢.

APPENDIX

26. *A Guide to the Cathedral Church of St. John the Divine, in the City of New York.* Published by the Layman's Club of the Cathedral Church of St. John the Divine, New York, N.Y. 75¢.

27. Reprints of the pictorial essay, *Life in the Middle Ages,* published in two parts in Life, April 7 and May 26, 1947.
    Available for 25¢ from the office Life at 9 Rockefeller Plaza, New York City. They contain several large color plates of windows of LeMans, Chartres and Bourges Cathedrals referred to in Bib. 1.

OTHER BOOKS OF INTEREST

28. Anderson, Robert Gordon. *Biography of a Cathedral.* New York, Longmans, Green and Company, 1945.
    A history of the Cathedral of Notre Dame in Paris, giving many details of the development of church architecture and decoration, liturgy, vestments, and civic life.

29. Adams, Henry. *Mont-Saint-Michel and Chartres.* Boston and New York, Houghton Mifflin Company, The Riverside Press, Cambridge, 1913.
    Chapter 8 is about Twelfth Century Glass, and Chapter 9 on Legendary Windows.

30. *Christmas—An American Annual of Christmas Literature and Art.* Minneapolis, Minn., Augsburg Publishing House, Volume 15. Edited by Randolph E. Haugan. $1.00.

31. Cram, Ralph Adams. *The Gothic Quest.* New York, Baker & Taylor Co., 1907.

32. Cram, Ralph Adams. *The Substance of Gothic.* Lowell Institute Lectures. Boston, Marshal Jones Co., 1917.

33. Cram, Ralph Adams. *The Catholic Church in Art.* New York, The Macmillan Company, 1930.

34. Eisen, G. A., and Kouchakji, F. *Glass.* New York, Wm. Rudge, 1927.

35. *Liturgical Arts.* A quarterly devoted to the arts of the Catholic Church. Published by Liturgical Arts Society, 10 Ferry St., Concord, N.H. $3.00 per year.

36. O'Reilly, Elizabeth Boyle. *How France Built Her Cathedrals.* New York, Harper & Brothers, 1921.

37. Tallmadge, Thomas E. *The Story of Architecture in America*. New York, W. W. Norton & Company, Inc., 1927.

38. Wallace, Dunlap. *Glass in the Old World*. New York, Scribner and Welford, 1880.

BOOKS ON SYMBOLISM

39. Baring, Gould S. *The Lives of the Saints*. Edinburgh, John Grant, 1914. 16 vols.

40. Butler, Alban. *Lives of the Fathers, Martyrs and Other Principal Saints*. London, Charles Dolman, 1847. 12 vols.

41. Conroy, Ellen. *Symbolism of Colour*. London, William Reder and Sons, 1921.

42. Fleming, Daniel Johnson. *Christian Symbols in a World Community*. New York, Friendship Press, 1940.
    This book contains 222 beautiful illustrations showing the use of the indigenous arts of Asia and Africa in the Christian churches of those lands. $2.00.

43. Fox-Davies, Arthur Charles. *A Complete Guide to Heraldry*. London, T. C. and E. C. Jack. 1929.

44. Geldart, Ernest. *A Manual of Church Decoration and Symbolism*. London and Oxford. A. R. Mowbray & Co., 1899.

45. Griffith, Helen Stuart. *The Sign Language of Our Faith*. New York, Morehouse Gorham Co., 1945.
    A handbook, written by a Pilgrim Aide at the Washington Cathedral; illustrated with over 60 drawings with notations as to their proper coloring. $1.50.

46. Stafford, Thomas Albert. *Christian Symbolism in the Evangelical Churches*. New York, Abingdon-Cokesbury Press, 1942.
    This book traces the historical background of Christian symbols, describes them, and explains the spiritual truths which have given them significance. Illustrated with many drawings by the author which are descriptive but can hardly be called artistic presentations of the symbols. $2.00.

47. Webber, F. R. *Church Symbolism*. Cleveland, Ohio, J. H. Jansen, 1927.

A 452 paged volume in which more than 500 symbols of early Christian, medieval, and contemporary architecture and decoration are illustrated and described. $7.50.

48. Webber, F. R. *The Small Church*. Cleveland, Ohio, J. H. Jansen, 1939.
How to build and furnish it, with some account of the improvement of existing buildings.

49. Wilson, Frank E. D.D. *An Outline of Christian Symbolism*. New York, Morehouse Gorham Co., 1938.
A small handbook illustrated with many line drawings and a few halftones sold for 40¢ at Episcopalian book stores.

Books on Design

50. Fry, Roger. *Vision and Design*. London, Chatto & Windus, 1920.

51. Kelly, Kathleen, B. *It's Fun to Design*. New York, Girl Scouts of the United States of America, 1944. Catalogue no. 20-308.
A handbook for girl scouts giving an elementary but graphic presentation of rhythm, basic forms in design, and the fundamentals of color and balance. Attractively illustrated. 75¢.

52. Knapp, Harriet E. *Design Approach to Crafts*. Sandusky, Ohio, Prang Company Publishers, a division of the American Crayon Company, 1945.
A concise but clear explanation of art structure with many beautiful illustrations.

53. de Lemos, Gordon. *A Handbook of Design*. New York, Educational Materials, Inc.
There are two fine chapters in this book on "How to Originate Designs" and "How to Use Color," in addition to hundreds of useful designs and suggestions for using them. $2.50.

54. Teaque, Walter Dorwin. *Design This Day*. New York, Harcourt, Brace and Company.
Deals with fundamentals which all designers should understand.

6. Notes on Plates

All illustrations are reproduced through the courtesy of the Artist or Stained Glass Studio named.

Frontispiece.
Making Frengosi Windows for a Worship Center, First Presbyterian Church, Englewood, New Jersey. Photograph by Coda, Englewood, N.J.

Plate 1. Single Medallions.
"The Battle at Lexington," "Religious Liberty," and "The Little Red School House," from cartoons for panels in Worcester Polytechnic Institute, by Wilbur Herbert Burnham, Boston, Mass. "Madonna and Child," and "The Clown," from glass medallions by Messrs. Reynolds, Francis & Rohnstock, Boston, Mass. "Team Play," from cartoon for detail in great west window, St. Mary's School, Glens Falls, N. Y. by Henry Lee Willet, Philadelphia, Pa.

Plate 2. Medallions in Plain Leaded Windows.
A portion of the "Village Blacksmith" window, in East Liberty Presbyterian Church, Pittsburgh, Pa. by Henry Lee Willet, Philadelphia, Pa. "Outward Bound—Homeward Bound," from cartoon by J. & R. Lamb, Tenafly, New Jersey.
Detail from cartoon for window in Grace Church, Providence, R.I. by Messrs. Reynolds, Francis & Rohnstock, Boston, Mass.

Plate 3a. Velvex Glass (reduced one half). A product of the Blue Ridge Glass Co. Marketed by Libby-Owens-Ford Co.

Plate 3b. Frengosi Medallions in a Portable Worship Center, designed by Ruth Case Almy and executed under her direction by children in the Junior Department of the First Presbyterian Church School, Englewood, N.J.

Plate 4. Small Windows with Medallions on Grisaille Background.
Side Chancel window in Saint George's Church, Maplewood, N.J. "The Annunciation" and "The Nativity," in Saint John's Episcopal Church, Florence, South Carolina. "Angel of Praise," in Trinity Church, Newton Centre, Mass. by Charles J. Connick Associates, Boston, Mass.

Plate 5. Small Windows with Medallions on Background of Geometric Design.

"Immortality," from colored sketch designed by Katharine Lamb for window in Ferncliff Mausoleum, N.Y. Executed by J. & R. Lamb Studios, Tenafly, N.J. "Blessed Are the Merciful," one of a series of clerestory windows in the Church of the Holy Name, New Bedford, Mass. by Charles J. Connick, Boston, Mass. "Gloria In Excelsis Deo," medallion window in Saint Bartholomew's Church, Hartsville, S. Carolina, by J. & R. Lamb Studios, Tenafly, N.J. Clerestory windows in Saint Joseph's Church, New Bedford, Mass., by Charles J. Connick, Boston, Mass.

Plate 6. Windows in Grisaille with Colored Strap Work.

Clerestory windows in Christ Church, Glendale, Ohio, by Charles J. Connick, Boston, Mass.

Plate 7. Windows in Ornamental Grisaille.

Choir stall window in Martin's Evangelical Lutheran Church, Casselton, N. Dakota. One of a series of ornamental windows in the Church of Saint John the Apostle, Leesburg, Va. Nave window, Saint Mary's Church, Cambridgeport, Mass. by Charles J. Connick Associates.

Plate 8. Modern Trends in Stained Glass.

"Pilgrim's Progress," a fragment of a window illustrating John Bunyan's Pilgrim's Progress, in Macartney Library, Geneva College, Beaver Falls, Pa., by Henry Lee Willet, Philadelphia, Pa. "Saint Francis," window in St. Mary's Church, Taylorville, Ill., by Emil Frei, Inc., St. Louis, Mo. "Ave Maria," cartoon for a window in the Lutheran Church, Bogota, N. J. designed by Katharine Lamb, executed by J. & R. Lamb Studios, Tenafly, N.J. "Morning Glories," decorated glass blocks, designed and executed by Rambusch Craftsmen, New York, City, N.Y. "Decorative Panel," medallion in abstract design by Emil Frei, St. Louis, Mo.

Plate 9. Medallion Windows with Background of Scrollwork and Geometric Design.

"Faith," from cartoon for window in Grace Church, Salem, Mass., by Messrs. Reynolds, Francis & Rohnstock, Boston, Mass. Aisle window in St. Joseph's Church, South Norwalk, Conn. by Pike Stained Glass Studios, Rochester, N.Y.

Plate 10. Medallion Windows with Bent Armatures.

Aisle window in Press Bay of the Cathedral of Saint John the Divine, New York, by the D'Ascenzo Studios, Philadelphia, Pa.

Plate 11. Selected Medallions.

"Saint Patrick," from a colored sketch by The Judson Studios, Los Angeles, California. "The Good Shepherd," memorial medallion in

APPENDIX

First Parish Church, Framingham Centre, Mass., by Charles J. Connick, Boston, Mass. "Ezekiel" from cartoon for medallion in Saint John the Evangelist Church, Rochester, N.Y. by Pike Stained Glass Studios, Rochester, N.Y.

Plate 12. Rose Window and Wheel Window.

"Angels of Praise and Prayer" from cartoon for window in Gary Memorial Methodist Episcopal Church, Wheaton, Ill. by Charles J. Connick, Boston, Mass.

"Great Teachers of the Arts," from cartoon for window in Shove Memorial Chapel, Colorado Springs, Colorado, by Messrs. Reynolds, Francis & Rohnstock, Boston, Mass.

Plate 13. Lancets with Tracery.

Clerestory window, Princeton University Chapel, Princeton, N.J. from a colored sketch by Pike Stained Glass Studios, Rochester, N.Y.

Plate 14. Large Figures with Background of Grisaille or Full Color.

Clerestory window in Chapel of the Monastery of Saint Mary and Saint John, Cambridge, Mass., by Charles J. Connick Associates, Boston, Mass.

"Golden Rule" window in Temple of Religion, Golden Gate International Exposition, San Francisco, California, by Cummings Studios, San Francisco, Cal.

"Saint Stephan" from cartoon for window in Saint James by the Sea Church, La Jolla, California, by The Judson Studios, Los Angeles, Cal.

Plate 15. Canopy Windows.

"Savonarola" and "Saint Bernard" from cartoons for portions of clerestory windows in Saint Martin's Church, Providence, R.I. by Messrs. Reynolds, Francis & Rohnstock, Boston, Mass.

"Saint Francis" from cartoon for window in Oneonta, N.Y. by Valentine d'Ogries, New Hope, Pa.

Plate 16.

Cartoon for a window in a modern automobile show room by Wilbur Herbert Burnham, Jr., Boston, Mass. "The Garden of Gethsemane," cartoon for portion of a window, one of a series, in the First Baptist Church, Richmond, Va., designed by Katharine Lamb, executed by J. & R. Lamb Studios, Tenafly, N.J. "The Carpenter's Son," cartoon for portion of a window, one of the same series.

7 · Notes on Figures

Figures 1 through 9:
   Sketches reproduced by courtesy of The Stained Glass Association of America.
Figures 10 through 18:
   Sketches by the author.
Figures 19, 20, 21, 22, 23, 24, 33:
   Reproduced from *The Dictionnaire Raisonne' de l' Architecture Française*, by E. Viollet-le-Duc.
Figures 25, 30, 33, 38:
   Reproduced from *Windows—A Book about Stained and Painted Glass*, by Lewis F. Day.
Figures 26, 27, 28, 29:
   Reproduced from *Adventures in Light and Color*, by Charles J. Connick, by courtesy of Random House, New York.
Figure 32:
   Border designs reproduced by courtesy of Wilbur H. Burnham, Messrs. Reynolds, Francis & Rohnstock, and The Cummings Stained Glass Studio; also from *Windows—A Book about Stained and Painted Glass*, by Lewis F. Day, and *A History of Design in Painted Glass*, by N. H. J. Westlake.
Figure 35:
   "Blessed James of Ulm," from a panel in glass by courtesy of John Riordan and Stephen Bridges, Cincinnati, Ohio.
Figure 39:
   Sketch by the author.
Figure 40, Cartoons available in the pattern supplement, and used by permission:
   A. "The Baby Moses," from a window in St. Peter and St. Paul Church, Hoboken, N.J., by courtesy of Pike Stained Glass Studios, Rochester, N.Y.
   B. "The Boy Samuel," by courtesy of John Riordan and Stephen Bridges, Cincinnati, Ohio.
   C. "Jesus and the Children," from a window in the Children's Chapel

[131]

of the Old South Church, Boston, Mass., by courtesy of Wilbur Herbert Burnham, Boston, Mass.

D. "The Crucifixion," from a window in St. Alban's Church, Westwood, Calif., by courtesy of The Judson Studios, Los Angeles, Calif.

E. "Noah's Ark," by courtesy of the same artists as in B.

F. "Crown of Thorns and Nails," by courtesy of the same artists as in E. and B.

G. "Children of Many Lands, (America, Holland, Alaska, Japan, India, American Indian, Africa, Russia) from windows in the First Methodist Church, Evanston, Ill., by courtesy of Charles J. Connick Associates, Boston, Mass.

H. "Indian at Sunset," by courtesy of the J. & R. Lamb Studio, Tenafly, N.J.

J. "Saint George and the Dragon," from a window in St. George's School Chapel, Newport, R.I., by courtesy of Messrs. Reynolds, Francis & Rohnstock, Boston, Mass.

K. "The Four Seasons," from a window in the Star of the Sea Church, San Francisco, Calif., by courtesy of the same artists as in G.

Index

INDEX

INDEX

Flux, 3, 63, 119
Frengosi, ix, xiii, xiv, 11-13, 38
Frengosi projects, 112-117
Frei, Emil, Inc., 129; Plate 8

Glass,
  annealing of, 7, 119
  Antique, 11, 72, 119
  blower, 71
  bricks, 18, 129; Plate 8
  coloring of, 3, 64, 71
  Crown, 72
  cutting of, 5, 20-21
  English Double-Rolled, 12, 109
  firing of, 7, 76
  flashed glass, 54, 71, 93
  Frengosi, xi
  Frengosi, coloring of, 23-26, 33-37, 41-42, 110
  Frengosi, permanence of, 41
  ingredients of, 3
  limitations of, 53-54
  making of, 3, 72
  Muff, 72
  Opalescent, 16, 19, 101-102
  origin of, 63-64
  painting of with black, 6, 13, 27-28, 46-47, 57, 65, 75, 81-82, 86, 88, 91, 94, 96, 98, 101
  raw, 57
  staining of, see Silver stain
  texture of, 11, 57
  Velvex, 11, 38, 57, 109, 128; Plate 3a
  Venetian, 72
Glazier, 65, 97, 119
Glazing, 8, 30, 111, 119
Goodhue, Bertram Grosvenor, 103
Gothic, 18, 67
  Early Period, 79, 86
  Late Period, 79, 92-96
  Middle Period, 79, 87-91
  Post, Period, 97-100
  revival of, in America, 103; in England, 100
Gregory of Tours, 65

Grisaille, 16, 40, 84-85, 87-88, 119, 128, 129; Plates 4, 6, 7

Halation, see Radiation
Heraldry, 90-91
Hurwitz, I., xi

Ironwork, 13, 51, 87. See also Crossbars

James, Betty G., xi
Japan dryer, 26
Jerome, 65
Jewels, 64, 93
Judson Studios, 129, 130, 132; Plates 11, 14; Figure 40D

Kaleidoscope, 14, 20, 112, 115-116, 119
Kiln, 75-76
King Philippe Auguste, 68

La Farge, John, 17, 101-102
Lamb, J&R Studios, 128, 129, 132; Plate 2, 5, 8, 16; Figure 40H
Lamb, Karl B., xi
Lamb, Katharine, xi, 129, 130; Plate 5, 8, 16
Lancets, 87, 119, 130; Plate 13
Leading, see Glazing
Leads, see Cames
Libby-Owens-Ford Co., 11, 109, 128
Limoges, 65
Lombardi, see Stained glass, lettering of

Mat, 7, 47
Medallions, 14; Plate 11
Metallic oxides, 3, 64, 71

INDEX

INDEX

INDEX

A. The Baby Moses

B. The Boy Samuel

C. Jesus and the Children

D. The Crucifixion

E. Noah's Ark

F. Crown of Thorns and Nails

FIG. 40 Reproductions of Cartoons Available in the Pattern Supplement

H. Indian at Sunset

G. Children of Many Lands

K. The Four Seasons

J. St. George and the Dragon

FIG. 40   (*Continued*)

NOTE the color keys.—Where two or more capital letters are used, the last letter indicates the basic color. All other letters indicate colors that modify the basic color, as: "GB" greenish blue; "BG" bluish green; "YW" yellowish white; "YB" light yellowish brown.

Leading is shown in gray; painting on the actual glass is marked in solid black.